A DISSENT ON BONHOEFFER

A DISSENT ON BONHOEFFER

David H. Hopper

THE WESTMINSTER PRESS
PHILADELPHIA

BOOK DESIGN BY DOROTHY E. JONES

PUBLISHED BY THE WESTMINSTER PRESS®
PHILADELPHIA, PENNSYLVANIA

PRINTED IN THE UNITED STATES OF AMERICA

Library of Congress Cataloging in Publication Data

Hopper, David.
   A dissent on Bonhoeffer.

   Includes bibliographical references and index.
   1. Bonhoeffer, Dietrich, 1906–1945. I. Title.
BX4827.B57H67   230′.092′4   75–22120
ISBN 0–664–20802–9

To Nancy,
   Sara, Kate, and Rachel

Contents

Preface

Dietrich Bonhoeffer's execution by the Nazis on April 9, 1945, was an event in Christian history. Although Bonhoeffer's execution for involvement in the German Resistance movement and his complicity in the plot to assassinate Hitler was not a major event in general history, it will nevertheless be long remembered by the Christian community. There were other Christians in the course of World War II who made sacrifices similar to that of Bonhoeffer, others who wrestled with the substance of faith and committed themselves to a course of action that resulted in their deaths. Most of the others are not as well known as Bonhoeffer—but through Bonhoeffer they will be remembered as well. The Christian community will continue to be inspired and nurtured by the witness of faith that was theirs.

In Bonhoeffer's case, however, something more is to be said. For Bonhoeffer was not only a witness to the faith; he also reflected upon the faith and wrote about his understanding of the substance of faith. Bonhoeffer was also a theologian. As theologian, he has had a significant impact on Christian thought in the years since World War II, when many of his writings were first published and his thought came into prominence. Much has been written about him as theologian—and this book proposes to offer still a further word. Unlike most of the recent analyses of Bonhoeffer's thought, however, this work offers a dissenting judgment about the enduring nature of his theological contribution.

This conclusion may perhaps cause some concern, some distress —especially among those who knew Bonhoeffer and have labored to make his thought known—also among those who have attempted to carry his thought farther. I do not suggest, with this analysis, that we will not continue to learn from his theological work. Rather, I am suggesting that many exaggerated claims have been made for that work and that these claims need to be challenged, if not corrected. They need to be challenged only for this reason: that something of the nature of the gospel may be at stake here. And if such is the case, I believe that Bonhoeffer himself would concur in this challenge.

It is to be hoped that this book will contribute to a better understanding of Bonhoeffer and his theology and also—as all theology should—to a better understanding of the gospel for our times.

A work such as this does not come to fruition without a pattern of indebtedness to others who helped in its realization. It is only proper and fitting to acknowledge this indebtedness.

I want to express special thanks to Eberhard Bethge for his openness to my varied inquiries on two separate occasions—in January of 1967 in St. Paul, Minnesota, and in June of 1970 at his home in Rengsdorf bei Neuwied/Rhein, Germany. Though the argument in this work may perhaps not meet with his general agreement, I am indebted to him for a deep appreciation of Bonhoeffer as a person—this, despite my critical judgments about his theology. If a man is known in part by his friends, Eberhard Bethge is an impressive witness to Bonhoeffer's humanity and Christian faith.

A 1969–1970 grant to Macalester College by the Ford Foundation enabled me to do a significant portion of the research on this project. The Foundation's efforts to develop the research potential of faculty persons in the humanities at smaller liberal arts colleges is greatly appreciated by me and also by my Macalester colleagues.

I am sure that many other faculty members at schools elsewhere across the nation echo our sentiments at this point.

I am indebted to Professor Herbert Richardson of the Institute of Christian Thought, Toronto, for encouragement and very helpful counsel and advice in the matter of publication. And I owe special thanks to Mrs. Carolynn Carlson for translating so patiently and ably my original manuscript into typescript.

My wife, Nancy, has said she does not want to hear from me on how all this would not have been possible without her strong support and encouragement, so I'll not say that. I *will* say, however, that when we very infrequently hassled over the time and effort that went into all this we invariably ended up laughing about it—and that I very much enjoyed and prize.

D. H. H.

Acknowledgments

Acknowledgment is made to the following publishers for use of their copyrighted materials:

Harper & Row, Publishers, Inc., for quotations from *Christ for Us in the Theology of Dietrich Bonhoeffer,* by John A. Phillips, copyright © 1967 by John A. Phillips.

Harper & Row, Publishers, Inc., and Wm. Collins Sons & Co., Ltd., for quotations from *No Rusty Swords,* by Dietrich Bonhoeffer, ed. by Edwin H. Robertson, tr. by Edwin H. Robertson and John Bowden, copyright © 1965 in the English translation; and from *The Way to Freedom,* from the Collected Works of Dietrich Bonhoeffer, ed. by Edwin H. Robertson, tr. by Edwin H. Robertson and John Bowden, copyright © 1966 in the English translation.

Lutterworth Press and Fortress Press, for quotations from *Reality and Faith: The Theological Legacy of Dietrich Bonhoeffer,* by Heinrich Ott, English translation copyright © 1972 by Lutterworth Press.

Macmillan Publishing Co., Inc., for quotations from *Dietrich Bonhoeffer: Theologian of Reality,* by André Dumas, copyright © 1971 by Macmillan Publishing Co., Inc., copyright © 1968 by Editions Labor et Fides, S.A. (Genève).

Macmillan Publishing Co., Inc., and SCM Press, Ltd., for quotations from *The Cost of Discipleship* (Second Edition), by Dietrich Bonhoeffer, copyright © SCM Press, Ltd., 1959; and from *Ethics,* by Dietrich Bonhoeffer, copyright © 1955 by SCM Press, Ltd., and Macmillan Publishing Co., Inc.; and from *Letters and Papers from Prison* (Revised, Enlarged Edition), by Dietrich Bonhoeffer, copyright © 1953, 1967, 1971 by SCM Press, Ltd.

⚭ 1 ⚭

The Impact of Bonhoeffer's Life and Thought

In a lecture delivered at Chicago Theological Seminary in January 1961, Eberhard Bethge, the friend and biographer of Dietrich Bonhoeffer, observed that although Bonhoeffer had "received great public attention . . . no clear-cut formula [had] yet appeared defining his contribution."[1] Bethge went on to say:

> The difficulty of grasping the meaning of Bonhoeffer's challenge [is to] be seen in Germany just after the war. Lutheran church representatives refused to accept him as a Christian martyr when they made the unpleasant discovery that this biblical scholar was a political plotter, but they eagerly reprinted and distributed his . . . church writings in camps all over the country. What about abroad? The ecumenical representatives immediately honored Bonhoeffer as a modern Christian martyr precisely because the German theologian died as an active resister, but they let the shadow of ignorance prevail as to whether or not Bonhoeffer was a theologian of some status [stature?]. . . . The answer still has to be given to the question: Admitting that the life of this man has spoken—can his theology make any impact?[2]

These words seem very strange to us today. Theologically the decade that followed upon Bethge's Chicago lectures might very well be described as "the Bonhoeffer decade." As a result, it is difficult to believe that Bethge's question, "Can his theology make any impact?" was ever asked. But in 1961 Bethge *did* ask that question—and justifiably so, it would seem. For Bonhoeffer's most provocative work, the collection entitled *Letters and Papers from Prison,* had already been in circulation for ten years and the *Ethics* for twelve; and Bethge felt that, up to 1961 at least, they had not received the kind of theological attention they deserved. Writing in 1967, when Bonhoeffer's name had become the dominant one in theological circles, Bethge ventured an explanation of the lag in theological appreciation that followed publication of Bonhoeffer's prison letters. He suggested that

> in Germany, when the *Letters and Papers from Prison* appeared, the second round of the Bultmann debate was in full swing; the voice of Gogarten was widely heard; Tillich, who had disappeared from the German scene, had reappeared; and Barth's doctrine of creation, his ethics and anthropology, had revealed the old master in new and broader dimensions. The questions of liberal theology had come vigorously to the fore again in 1952 after the great testing of dialectical theology and the time of a new confessional awareness [a reference to the German church struggle against Nazi domination]. Into this situation Bonhoeffer's brief notes came too late for the academic discussion. They had, as it were, to consent immediately to perform the services of secondary weapons in the respective armories, which had already been equipped with fixed types of weapons. He who had become bored with Barth found his ammunition in [Bonhoeffer's] catch phrase "posi-.ivism of revelation." He who advocated the existential interpretation felt himself supported by . . . [Bonhoeffer's] "non-religious interpreta-tion." . . . He who despaired of the concrete church discovered the "world come of age" and saw the possibility of adopting an atheistic world view in the name of Bonhoeffer's "theology of the cross." In short, the time was not favorable for Bonhoeffer's fragments to speak in their own right.[3]

The situation that Bethge deplored in 1961 changed radically in the subsequent few years. In 1959, Jürgen Moltmann had published an analysis of Bonhoeffer's Christology in relation to his ethics,[4] and John Godsey in 1960 and Hanfried Müller in 1961 published full-length studies of Bonhoeffer's theology.[5] But it was not until John A. T. Robinson's *Honest to God* (1963)[6] signaled a change in the theological ethos that Bonhoeffer's thought began to claim distinctive prominence.[7] Robinson, a bishop of the Church of England and a respected New Testament scholar, gave frank expression to his own disaffection with and doubt about traditional theological formulations. The little treatise in which he expressed these views, *Honest to God,* attracted worldwide attention. Making use of the thought of Paul Tillich, Rudolf Bultmann, and Dietrich Bonhoeffer, Robinson established the antipodal alternative to the confessionalism that had emerged out of the struggle against National Socialism in Germany. Bonhoeffer appeared in a new light as one who, having steadfastly opposed Nazi inhumanity, offered a possibility of moving beyond the "neo-orthodoxy" of Barth and the existential sobriety of Bultmann in the direction of a Christian humanism inspired by the vision of Jesus as "the man for others." The debate that followed the publication of Robinson's book helped to focus attention on Bonhoeffer's theology, and a new generation of theologians began its quest for theological identity.

In the same year that Robinson's controversial treatise appeared, Paul van Buren, on the American scene, published a provocative book entitled *The Secular Meaning of the Gospel.*[8] Though van Buren, in this work, came to the task of theologizing out of the philosophical school of linguistic analysis, the theological purpose he defined was identical with that spelled out by Bonhoeffer in his prison letters, i.e., the statement of a "non-religious interpretation of biblical concepts." In the dedication of his book van Buren made clear his debt to Bonhoeffer; and still later, in a 1967 article, he declared that nothing short of a new world view was implied in Bonhoeffer's paradoxical formula according to which the present-day Christian is called to live "with God without God."[9]

Some two years after the appearance of Robinson's best seller and van Buren's widely hailed work, Harvey Cox came forth with still another theological-journalistic triumph: *The Secular City.*[10] Here again, despite some effort by Cox to discuss theological alternatives, the major influence discernible in the work was Bonhoeffer.[11] Like van Buren, Cox in *The Secular City* defined his major task as a restatement of Christian faith that, at one and the same time, would free faith from the encrustations of "religion" and "metaphysics" (negative terms in Bonhoeffer's prison letters) and make common cause with a "profane" and "pragmatic" humanism.[12] In a subsequent article Cox, like van Buren, set forth what he regarded as Bonhoeffer's contributions to the current theological scene. He described an interview with twelve visiting German theologians who asked Cox to outline the major motifs making up contemporary American theology. After some hesitation Cox ventured a description of four trends that one of his visitors immediately identified as themes in Bonhoeffer's thought. Cox agreed with the observation and then, in the article, asserted:

> We cannot yet "move beyond" him because we have not yet faced his challenge seriously. His uncanny capacity to uncover the hidden skeletons in the closets of theology and to see issues coming around the corner means that we have not shaken him. It may be embarrassing to assign readings from someone who has already been written up in a photo essay by *Life,* but as one American theologian put it, "We have to continue studying Bonhoeffer even though 'he is a fad.' "[13]

Reference to the Bonhoeffer "fad" indicates how suddenly things had changed with regard to the attention focused on Bonhoeffer. In the 1950's, as Bethge described it, Bonhoeffer's writings were used chiefly as secondary weapons in the theological controversies revolving around other names and figures. But in the mid-1960's, as Cox viewed the situation, theologians had become concerned about being caught up in a "Bonhoeffer fad." Certainly occasion for concern was given at the time by the "death of God" theology, which captured the headlines in many secular weeklies and newspapers during late 1964 and 1965. Identified chiefly with the names of William Hamilton and Thomas J. J. Altizer, the "death of God" theology represented a repudiation of the traditional conception of God and pressed the point that God's presence was no longer a reality in the lives of most contemporary Christians, that if there ever was a God he had now withdrawn from the human scene and that the duty of Christians was to seek enrichment of life in interpersonal relations. Altizer's brand of the "death of God" theology varied in important respects from Hamilton's and was more inclined toward metaphysics (Hegel) and mysticism. However, Hamilton, the more articulate and understandable of the two, looked especially to the figures of Dostoevsky and Bonhoeffer as inspiration for his own "death of God" formulations. Hamilton described his point of view in the following terms:

> Today we need to look at the Reformation in a third sense, no more or less true than the earlier approaches [i.e., "autonomous religious personality," and "the righteous God"], but perhaps needing special emphasis just now and fitting new experiences in both church and world. This approach is more ethical than psychological or theological, and its focus is not on the free personality or on justification by faith, but on the movement from the cloister to the world. Here I reflect the thought of the later Bonhoeffer. My Protestant has no God, has no faith in God, and affirms both the death of God and the death of all forms of theism. Even so, he is not primarily a man of negation, for if there is a movement away from God and religion, there is the more important movement into, for, toward the world, worldly life, and the neighbor as the bearer of the worldly Jesus.[14]

Hamilton's use of Bonhoeffer's thought in the cause of this new but short-lived theological movement was not well received by some of Bonhoeffer's close friends and interpreters. Bethge in a visit to the United States in 1966–1967 frequently expressed himself in opposition to what he felt was a loose adaptation of Bonhoeffer's thought. In interviews and lectures repeated across the country, Bethge pointed out that "one sentence in [Bonhoeffer's] writing, 'Before God, we have to live today without God,' has been 'distorted' by some theologians to say, 'We have to live today without God.' "[15] And Paul Lehmann, a close American friend of Bonhoeffer, described Hamilton's use of Bonhoeffer's concept of a "world come of age" as a "careless dissemination of a half-truth" and labeled his exposition of Bonhoeffer's thought as "confusion worse confounded."[16]

Nevertheless the change in the theological landscape that had taken place in the few years since 1961—albeit with some distor-

tion and misuse of Bonhoeffer's thought—was impressive. Jaroslav
Pelikan helped to describe this change when, in a 1967 review, he
observed:

> The brightest new star of recent Protestant theology is Dietrich Bon-
> hoeffer. . . . Bonhoeffer began to address a world audience only after
> his death . . . but . . . [he] has addressed the world also through his
> death, for he was hanged by the Nazis on April 9, 1945, for his part
> in the plot of July 20, 1944, to assassinate Hitler. Bonhoeffer was just
> thirty-nine when he was murdered. Thus, had he lived, he would only
> now be in his prime as a scholar and thinker. Yet in the two decades
> since his death his writings, letters, sermons, diaries, and lecture notes
> have been collected, published, and studied in Europe and America.
> College students who insist that they are not very religious stay away
> from Chapel and read Bonhoeffer; theological students who are bored
> by traditional dogmatics have formed little Bonhoeffer coteries at vari-
> ous seminaries; and a couple of pages from his *Letters and Papers from
> Prison* have become, quite distortedly, the program of those who an-
> nounce "the death of God."[17]

The conceptual stimulus behind this surge of interest in Bonhoeffer was a number of undeveloped ideas that Bonhoeffer penned
to his friend Eberhard Bethge from his prison cell in the year prior
to his execution. For example, van Buren and Cox sought chiefly
to develop Bonhoeffer's idea of a "non-religious interpretation of
biblical concepts" or, as Bonhoeffer expressed it at one point,
"religionless Christianity." Most interpreters made wide use of his
concept of a "world come of age," a world in which human need
was no longer seen as the ground of man's relationship to God.
This thought, in fact, underlay Bonhoeffer's dictum that "Before
God and with God we live without God."[18] Bonhoeffer's embrace
of the nondoctrinaire "secular" man and his picture of Jesus as
"the man for others" also spurred theologians to try to bring his
ideas to a fuller development.

But the provocative thoughts contained in the prison letters
were not the only basis of Bonhoeffer's appeal. As both Bethge and
Pelikan suggest, his life had an especially profound impact upon
many, both inside and outside the Christian community. This im-

pact seemingly grew with the years. The waning of the cold war during the 1960's allowed greater political movement; and, in theological circles, political theology came increasingly to the fore. Bonhoeffer's example of committed political involvement gave support to those who now saw in the political arena the call to Christian discipleship. In Europe the "Christian-Marxist dialogue" became a much-publicized phenomenon as Marxists and Christians entered into discussion about the realities of the human condition.[19] Jürgen Moltmann's politically oriented "theology of hope" came quickly to prominence and mirrored Bonhoeffer's criticism of the traditional Lutheran division of life into "religious" and "secular" spheres. Though some would not describe Bonhoeffer's influence upon Moltmann as explicit,[20] it can be said that Bonhoeffer helped bring about a more earnest theological confrontation with the political question.

On the American scene, opposition to the American involvement in the Vietnam war greatly extended an appreciation for Bonhoeffer's life and its pattern of political opposition. In a trenchant discussion of the subject, "Political Theology in the Crossfire,"[21] Roger Shinn, professor of social ethics at Union Theological Seminary, noted that two vastly different approaches to the political question are to be found in the Christian tradition. One he typified with a quote from Max Weber: "He who seeks the salvation of the soul, of his own and others, should not seek it along the avenue of politics, for the quite different tasks of politics can only be solved by violence."[22] Shinn then wrote:

> An opposing interpretation, more appealing to our time, has been stated by Dietrich Bonhoeffer:
> "It is only by living completely in this world that one learns to believe. One must abandon every attempt to make something of oneself, whether it be a saint, a converted sinner, a churchman (the priestly type, so-called), a righteous man or an unrighteous one, a sick man or a healthy one. This is what I mean by worldliness—taking life in one's stride, with all its duties and problems, its successes and failures, its experiences, and helplessnesses. It is in such a life that we throw ourselves utterly in the arms of God and participate in his sufferings

in the world and watch with Christ in Gethsemane."

Bonhoeffer wrote that statement on July 21, 1944, after receiving news of the failure of the attempted assassination of Hitler on July 20. His own role in the conspiracy heightens the contrast between his belief and the ethic described by Max Weber. The ethic of Bonhoeffer, especially as incarnated in his life, has powerful appeal to the contemporary Christian conscience.[23]

Though Shinn does not note this in his discussion, an equivalent occasion was fundamental to an appreciation of the "powerful appeal" of Bonhoeffer's example. And in the minds of many upon the American theological scene an equivalent occasion was found in the Vietnam war. Although it is clear that American fascination with Bonhoeffer and the new kinds of theological questions he posed were already in full swing prior to the escalation of the Vietnam war, that event very much spread Bonhoeffer's influence at a theological "grass roots" level among pastors and Christian laymen, both young and old. The widespread feeling that the war in Southeast Asia was "immoral," the fervor of the resistance to the war, characterizations of the United States Government as oppressive or "proto-fascist,"[24] the acceptance of conspiratorial patterns as necessary expressions of Christian opposition to the war: these aspects of American resistance to the war found a special kind of reinforcement in the Bonhoeffer image and resulted in a widespread identification with the life and thought of the later Bonhoeffer. Thus, although a very early acceptance of Bonhoeffer's martyrdom was apparent in the English-speaking world, the "discovery" of Bonhoeffer's prison letters, followed then by the Vietnam situation and an even deeper identification with Bonhoeffer's personal witness, established him as *the* major influence on the American theological scene during the late 1960's.[25]

Overall, both in Europe and America, these two dimensions of Bonhoeffer's influence, his stimulating theological statement and his political involvement, give warrant for describing the past ten or so years of theological endeavor as "the Bonhoeffer decade." The name of no other theologian rivals that of Bonhoeffer in breadth of influence during these years. In fact, enthusiasm for

Bonhoeffer's contribution during this period brought forth frequent claims of an "epochal" turning point in Christian thought. Already we have noted Harvey Cox's estimate of Bonhoeffer's contribution—his suggestion in late 1965 that in the twenty years that followed World War II, theology had not "moved beyond" Bonhoeffer nor seriously faced his challenge. William Kuhns, a Catholic interpreter, wrote in 1967:

> As a thinker . . . and as a deeply spiritual man, but above all as the union of both, Bonhoeffer has offered the Church a wealth of self-understanding, and the point of departure for a large-scale form of critical introspection. Indeed, it is impossible, in the final analysis, to estimate the real value of the man's integrity of thought and life. . . . It is indeed possible that Bonhoeffer, with his life and finally with his martyrdom, has provided the epitaph to a long and ultimately sterile tradition of theology in which the theologian's personal life matters little.[26]

John A. Phillips, another interpreter, asserted:

> His work is and must remain fragmentary—[but it affords us] a glimpse of "the way in which the whole was planned and conceived, and of what material he was building with—or should have used had he lived." To have known that his work provided us with such a glimpse and has made a lasting contribution to the renewal of theology and the disclosure of "Christ for us today" would have gratified him deeply. Our task is to strike our tents and to go forth into the region which he sketched crudely but did not live to enter.[27]

And Heinrich Ott, the man who succeeded to Karl Barth's chair of theology at Basel, also defined Bonhoeffer's contribution in epochal terms:

> Our thesis is that Bonhoeffer stands at the focal point of all the important questions discussed today by theology, or at least by systematic theology, and that he does so in such a way that his contribution is sometimes still something to be awaited, a contribution to which expression and relevant pointedness would have to be given by interpretation of his work. . . . In this sense we believe that we can see in him the most radical and modern Protestant thinker of our time.[28]

In assessing these claims for Bonhoeffer's impact on theology, one notes that—apart from the assertion of an "epochal" character for this contribution—no consensus regarding that contribution emerges. For Kuhns, Bonhoeffer's significance lies in his integration of life and thought. For Phillips it is represented by his opening up of a new, roughly charted theological future. For Ott it is Bonhoeffer's encompassing of all the most profound theological questions, especially the question about "reality." Certainly Bonhoeffer has stirred and moved many people in many different ways. But to have noted this phenomenon is by no means to have established the precise nature of Bonhoeffer's enduring theological contribution. That is a question which remains to be examined.

∿ 2 ∿

The Questions
of Stature and
Continuity of Thought

In his 1961 Chicago lectures Eberhard Bethge actually posed two different questions. There is the question: "Can [Bonhoeffer's] theology make any impact?"—a question that, as suggested, must be answered in a very affirmative way. Bonhoeffer's impact has been exceedingly widespread and the problems he posed in his later thought have commanded the attention of a number of the new generation of theologians.

But a second question—which Bethge may not have distinguished from the first—concerns Bonhoeffer's stature as a theologian. In his Chicago lectures Bethge accused "ecumenical representatives" of recognizing the character of Bonhoeffer's martyrdom but of then allowing "the shadow of ignorance" to prevail as to whether Bonhoeffer was a theologian of some stature. This question about Bonhoeffer's stature cannot be answered in the same unequivocal way that the first question was answered, in spite of the acclaim that Bonhoeffer's work has received from most recent interpreters of his thought. An answer to the question of stature in the theological sphere is not to be determined on the basis of extensive impact alone. It is related to such other factors as continuity of thought, depth of insight, ability to stimulate long-term results in theological conceptualization, and also the capacity to inform and enrich the life of the believing community.[1] When these other considerations are brought to bear upon an assessment of Bonhoeffer's theological contribution, it would seem that the declarations of Bonhoeffer's epochal stature are somewhat premature. Some of these considerations, such as the capacity of Bonhoeffer's theology to yield long-term results in theological conceptualization, or to help sustain the life of the church, demand greater historical perspective than we presently possess. However, on the two matters of continuity and depth of insight a fair amount of opinion has already been expressed. Unfortunately, the discussion up to this point has not always taken the form of real dialogue, but it has often manifested itself in assertive claims and declarations. In part at least, this may be a result of the fact that determinative points at issue have not always been clearly articulated and directly addressed.[2] What seems to have taken place is that one dominant view of Bonhoeffer's theological stature has simply superseded another without, at points, the kind of careful exchange one might expect. One suspects, rather, that a shift in the spirit of the times —reflected, for example, by a surge of enthusiasm for "new frontiers in theology" and "new theology"[3]—had an important role to play in a sudden alteration of theological concerns which helped to bring Bonhoeffer's thought to the fore.

To sharpen the statement of the problem: what Bethge deplored in the situation of 1961, i.e., "the shadow of ignorance" surrounding the question of Bonhoeffer's theological stature, was in part at least a reflection of Bethge's own dissatisfaction with a fairly early and widespread negative judgment on this matter. Such a judgment, for example, was expressed by a German graduate student, Eckhard Minthe, who, in speaking to an American audience in the spring of 1961, declared:

> The attempt to systematize Bonhoeffer's thought and then to work out its application is doomed from the start to failure, for his ideas were impulsive reactions to a peculiar set of circumstances. They are so impetuous and so conditioned by the situation in which Bonhoeffer found himself that one could almost speak of them as prophetic oracles.[4]

Minthe's statement of opinion parallels the view of another, better-known theological figure. In 1952, a year after publication of the original German edition of *Letters and Papers from Prison,* Karl Barth described Bonhoeffer's theological stature in the following manner:

> As always with Bonhoeffer, one is faced by a peculiar difficulty. He was —how shall I put it?—an impulsive visionary thinker who was suddenly seized by an idea to which he gave lively form, and then after a time he called a halt (one never knew whether it was final or temporary) with some provisional last point or other. Was this not the case with *The Cost of Discipleship?* Did he not also for a time have liturgical impulses?—And how was it with the "Mandates" of his *Ethics*—Do we not always expect him to be clearer and more concise in some other context, either by withdrawing what he said, or by going even further?[5]

On occasion, Barth was able to heap high praise on aspects of Bonhoeffer's work. In the same letter quoted above he asserted: "I always perused his earlier writings, especially those which apparently, or in reality, said things which were not at once clear to me, with the thought that—when they were seen round some other corner—he might be right."[6] But Barth's estimate of Bonhoeffer as impulsive and unpredictable certainly calls into question the systematic substance of Bonhoeffer's theological contribution and clearly contests the later claim of an "epochal role" for his theology.

Some may ask, of course, whether the insistence upon systematic coherence and development in a man's thought is really of crucial significance. For many perhaps it is not. Perhaps it is possible for some to claim the prophetic oracle, the flash of insight, the undeveloped thought, as sufficient ground for defining a pivotal turning point in Christian thought. But for the most part, in theology as well as in other disciplines, mature development of concepts, the clear revision or abandonment—with reason—of earlier viewpoints continue to represent an essential feature of substantive and enduring thought. It has, of course, been argued—and likely will continue to be—that Bonhoeffer's theological career was cut off in the bud, that his involvement in life simply did not permit this kind of scholarly, systematic exposition.[7] One certainly must take note of this qualifying circumstance and allow it to moderate any final judgment. One can well imagine that had Bonhoeffer lived, he would have made a major systematic contribution to the post– World War II theological world. But such a supposition is really only speculative. What we have at our disposal are only Bon- hoeffer's extant works—and it is about these that we must ask the question whether they represent enough to justify the sorts of claims that have been made for his theology. The main thrust of the argument which follows is that they do not, and that in fact Bonhoeffer's thought was troubled by some long-standing personal questions which received different answers at different points in his life and which help to explain some of the unexpected turns in his thinking. In short, there is room also for some theological reserve on Bonhoeffer, as well as exuberant enthusiasm.

In point of fact, the more positive and now dominant appraisal of Bonhoeffer was beginning to take shape about the time of Beth- ge's 1961 Chicago lectures. This alternative appraisal was built around the assertion that Bonhoeffer's thought was *not* impulsive as Barth had suggested, but rather that it was grounded in some basic unifying themes and concerns discernible throughout the course of his theological career. It is clear that Bethge himself was long associated with this estimate of Bonhoeffer's work, but sup- port from other quarters was needed to give currency to the argu- ment. This support began to emerge in the middle and late 1950's. In 1955, Gerhard Ebeling, a respected younger theologian and onetime student of Bonhoeffer, opened the breach with the earlier assessment by Barth and others when he asserted that Bonhoeffer's later concept of a "non-religious interpretation of biblical con- cepts" was rooted in certain long-standing theological presupposi- tions which were more than mere personal whim and which repre- sented the *sine qua non* of theological thinking itself.[8] Another key work in this emerging reassessment was Jürgen Moltmann's 1959 study of the social ethics of Bonhoeffer, a work entitled *The Lord-*

ship of Christ and Human Society.[9] In this discussion Moltmann
made a point of major importance when he argued that there was
a pattern of continuous development in Bonhoeffer's thought. As
Moltmann expressed it:

> In his earlier writings, Bonhoeffer was preoccupied with the sociology
> of the church and with the consequences of faith in the presence of
> Christ in his church, with "Christ existing as Christian community,"
> and with the distinctive nature of the community in discipleship. In
> *Ethics,* however, his horizons are broadened to include the Lordship
> of Christ not only in the church, but also in the world. His concern
> now, obviously, is with the presence of Christ in the center and in the
> fulness of life. He seeks to view every sphere of life as part of the world
> reconciled in Christ with God. In noting this change we do not mean
> to imply a breach in Bonhoeffer's work as a whole. Nor will it be
> possible to quote his latest thinking against his earlier theological es-
> says. Rather, we should draw the conclusion that it was the theology
> of the earlier writings, the "ethical social transcendence of God," the
> "entering of God into reality" and the "vicarious action of Christ,"
> which now prove their worth when applied to other themes.[10]

What Moltmann offered in this brief statement came to represent the emerging consensus of subsequent Bonhoeffer scholarship
—a field of growing theological investigation in the decade of the
1960's. This is not to suggest that all interpreters of Bonhoeffer's
thought were agreed at all points; in fact, it is very important to
take note—as we shall be doing—of the striking differences among
leading Bonhoeffer interpreters. But, in the main, the following two
points came to represent the common ground of the new assessment: first, that Bonhoeffer, throughout his theological work, was
profoundly Christological in his theological concern and secondly,
that the scope of his vision was ever more broadly encompassing
over the years. It now was commonly argued that to understand
properly the nature and content of the *Letters and Papers from
Prison* one had to interpret them in the context of Bonhoeffer's
earlier writings and be cognizant of his developing and increasingly
perceptive grasp of reality as he became more and more involved
in the life of the world. Thus, Eberhard Bethge's definitive biogra-

phy is entitled "Dietrich Bonhoeffer: Theologian, Christian, Contemporary,"[11] suggesting that the titles of "theologian," "Christian," "contemporary" represent progressive stages in Bonhoeffer's
life, each stage taking up the substance of the previous stage and
adding commitment and greater involvement, along with depth of
insight.

In 1961 an East German interpreter, Hanfried Müller, underlined one aspect of this new appraisal of Bonhoeffer in the title of
his book, "From the Church to the World."[12] Müller's study is an
interesting effort to place Bonhoeffer in a Marxist-Christian frame
of reference, and he sketches Bonhoeffer's development in terms of
a changing awareness of the social and political situation. Müller
argued that the limitations of Bonhoeffer's earlier thought were
essentially to be understood as a result of the social and political
conditions under which he lived,[13] but that in the end he gained a
vision of a new day and a new social order in which the Word of
God would have a continuing, positive role to play. Müller said of
Bonhoeffer:

> [The way he trod] leads from the old to the new, from an affirmed past
> into an affirmed future. Because this way was so consistent, because its
> inner necessity is demonstrable at almost every stage, therefore it can
> serve as a model for the bourgeois Christian of our time. It does not
> depart from the gospel. It does not reject the middle class, but opens
> the eyes of the bourgeoisie to new, great tasks. It gives the bourgeois
> man as Christian the freedom to cooperate in the tasks which a new
> time poses.[14]

Such an account of Bonhoeffer's movement of broadening commitment, from the clearly demarcated boundaries of the Confessing Church in Germany to a new "religionless" world, proved to
be a persuasive pattern for interpreting the main lines of Bonhoeffer's thought, though elements of Müller's Marxist interpretation were frequently challenged. It was generally agreed that the
dynamic source of Bonhoeffer's theology was his Christological
concern, his firm rootage in the gospel, conjoined with his awareness of the realities of the world.

This reappraisal of Bonhoeffer, which emerged in the German-speaking world, was paralleled by a similar development in the English-speaking world when John Godsey published his well-received study *The Theology of Dietrich Bonhoeffer,*[15] which, like Müller's work, served both as an exposition of Bonhoeffer's thought as a whole and an interpretation of his theological development. Godsey struck many of the same notes as Moltmann and Müller in his assessment of Bonhoeffer's contribution. Godsey declared: "For Bonhoeffer theology was essentially Christology."[16] Also, Godsey marked off three stages in the development of Bonhoeffer's thought:

> During the first period his thought centered on *Jesus Christ as the revelational reality of the Church.* During the second period his emphasis was upon *Jesus Christ as the Lord over the Church.* In the third period Bonhoeffer concentrated his attention upon *Jesus Christ as the Lord over the world.*[17]

And he made a point of insisting that in this pattern of development Bonhoeffer did not abandon the doctrine of the church but anticipated its presence and function even in a religionless world.[18]

These patterns of reappraisal predate Bethge's Chicago lectures; but they do not invalidate Bethge's 1961 concern on this point. These voices were only beginning to be heard and it was not until the pivotal year of 1963—with John A. T. Robinson's *Honest to God* and Paul van Buren's *The Secular Meaning of the Gospel*—that the real surge of enthusiasm for Bonhoeffer's new theological perspective began to take hold. Thereafter, and on up to the present time, voices of support for Bonhoeffer's pivotal significance have consistently been heard, most of them accepting and underlining the Christocentric, yet ever more realistic and inclusive character of Bonhoeffer's thought.

Some of these subsequent interpretations deserve scrutiny because in the process of "fixing" the new appraisal of Bonhoeffer they also raise interesting questions about aspects of Bonhoeffer's thought and the adequacy of some of the earlier statements in the new appraisal. For example, John A. Phillips, in his 1967 study

Christ for Us in the Theology of Dietrich Bonhoeffer, added his support for the new assessment, underlining the major points of Christological focus and the movement from church to world. Explicitly concurring with Müller and Godsey on the point of Christological focus, Phillips asserts:

> Bonhoeffer's emphasis on Christology, particularly on a Christology which exhibited certain definite and constant tendencies, *is* a basic clue to his thinking. One cannot escape it in any assessment, and it has been adopted in this study as the light which can illuminate the dark places, narrow passes, and turnings of Bonhoeffer's path. . . . It will be our task to uncover the Christological motivation for the various shifts in Bonhoeffer's concern. Bethge has described this motivation as "the quest for the concretion of the revelation," by which he means that Bonhoeffer struggled, throughout his life, to give adequate expression to his conviction that the revelation of God in Jesus Christ was visible, tangible, concrete, apprehensible by all men. . . . Bonhoeffer's Christology *developed;* to say that it was a constant motif of his thought does not mean that it remained an *idée fixe* by which he measured the utterances of fifteen years. His theology issued from the tension, we shall argue, between unreconciled elements in its Christological centre.[19]

For Phillips it is the Christological concern which was absolutely basic to the pattern of Bonhoeffer's theological development and provided the stimulus for important changes that Phillips identifies in Bonhoeffer's later thought. Especially does Phillips note the abandonment of Bonhoeffer's early ecclesiological Christology in favor of what he describes as a "new Christology," one reaching out simultaneously to both the individual and the world. This "new Christology," Phillips asserts, first emerged in Bonhoeffer's 1933 Berlin lectures on Christology. About these lectures, Phillips declares:

> Bonhoeffer [here] has moved beyond the limitations of "Christ existing as the church" to a conception of the person of Christ as both center and boundary of the individual believer. He has located the central Christological problem not in the relationship of God to Jesus nor of Jesus to the church, but in the manner in which Jesus is in the world, for others. Revelation becomes the act in which Christ, who comes to

me in Word, Sacrament, and Community, the humiliated God-Man whose total existence is for me, is confessed as God. As the absolutely transcendent, he stands free from me on the boundary and at the center of my existence; in his transcendence, I find my center and my boundary.[20]

According to Phillips, this promising statement of new themes in Bonhoeffer's Christology was kept from further immediate development by Bonhoeffer's deepening involvement in the German church struggle against the Nazis and "German Christians."[21] Phillips suggests that the intensity of that struggle caused Bonhoeffer to slip into an unfortunate church-world antithesis which temporarily stayed the development of Bonhoeffer's new, world-affirming Christology sketched out in the 1933 lectures. Phillips maintains that the 1936–1937 work, *The Cost of Discipleship,* though reflecting Bonhoeffer's consistent demand for concrete, obedient existence, was essentially a response to the force of Nazi persecution and reflected a situation in which Bonhoeffer became, but only temporarily, a spokesman for "a 'boundary' between Christ and the world, a barrier set not by Christ but by the world which rejects him."[22] In *The Cost of Discipleship,* Phillips concludes, the word "transcendence" means "primarily freedom from the world."[23] Later, however, Bonhoeffer, in Phillips' view, turned from this "breach with the world" to reclaim it for Christ.[24]

In regard to Godsey's earlier linking of Christology and ecclesiology and Godsey's assertion that the two themes remain basic features of Bonhoeffer's thought through *Letters and Papers from Prison,* Phillips says: "The central difficulty in . . . Godsey's interpretation seems to be [his] choice of ecclesiology as a vantage point. Godsey can hold Bonhoeffer's position together as a thoroughgoing ecclesiology only by dismissing the very important and significant final criticism of the church and of Barth, whom Bonhoeffer identified with its mistakes."[25] Phillips goes on to assert: "Whatever Bonhoeffer was concerned with in the *Ethics* and the prison letters, it was *not* primarily ecclesiology."[26]

At about the same time as Phillips' work appeared, Heinrich Ott published an analysis of Bonhoeffer's thought that also asserted the

theme of continuity.[27] Ott's work parallels Phillips' analysis at
some points. Ott insists that Bonhoeffer's work is bound together
by two unifying themes, one of which is Christology.[28] He, like
Phillips, argues for the special significance of the 1933 Christology
lectures in affirming and projecting a world-embracing Christology, which Ott speaks of as a "universalist" or, more commonly,
an "ontological Christology." Unlike Phillips, however, Ott does
not note a withdrawal from this universalist Christology in *The
Cost of Discipleship;* rather, he insists on its constancy throughout
Bonhoeffer's thought, its fullest expression coming in *Ethics* and
in *Letters and Papers from Prison.*[29] Ott further states that "[Bon-
hoeffer's] thought is anti-individualist throughout"[30] and that there
is no abandonment of the concept of the church over the course
of Bonhoeffer's theological work. In discussing Bonhoeffer's
ecumenical significance, Ott asserts:

> Significant above all here is the thought of the *Sanctorum Communio,*
> the church as the fellowship of believers and more than the mere sum
> of them, the thought with which Bonhoeffer dealt in detail in his
> doctorate and in his inaugural dissertation, and which, we can add, he
> never recanted or essentially modified in later time, and of which we
> can also find such examples directly or indirectly in his late utter-
> ances.[31]

Obviously Ott's insistence on the continuity of Bonhoeffer's ecclesiological interest represents a point shared with Moltmann, Godsey,
and Bethge but stands in opposition to the views of Müller and
Phillips.[32]

Ott insists that Bonhoeffer's Christological concern cannot be
viewed in isolation. He suggests that this theme is conjoined with
a second theme that runs throughout Bonhoeffer's thought and
helps to chart the direction of his theological development. This
second theme may be termed the "reality theme." Ott speaks at one
point as though this reality theme was actually Bonhoeffer's sole
concern. For example, in a discussion of the importance of Jer., ch.
45, for an understanding of Bonhoeffer's prison experience, Ott
states:

We have illuminated . . . the *one* theme of his life's history and life's work. For this seems to me to run through his thought from beginning to end, the uncompromisingly honest endeavor to look in the face the concreteness of the reality lived and to be lived by us, to stand by it without subtraction, without speculative addition, without allowing himself to be misled by artificial theories and mere words which lack equivalent value in the experience of reality.[33]

Ott then, however, goes on to speak of two "inescapabilities" as dimensions of Bonhoeffer's perception of reality:

If God lives and if Jesus Christ is his final word, then this must be as inescapable as life itself. To fail to see or to deny the inescapability of the situation, to seek to break out of it, would have been for Bonhoeffer a flight into insincerity. . . . And so for Bonhoeffer . . . the two inescapabilities, the inescapability of God [Christology] and the inescapability of the situation, converged. So reality became his keyword, his motto, the word which stood for his problems. The problems he thus sensed appear in varied forms in the course of his pilgrimage, but in the last resort it is always the same.[34]

Whereas Phillips tended to account for the movement in Bonhoeffer's thought as an expression of "the tension . . . between unreconciled elements in its Christological center" and Müller explained it as a result of Bonhoeffer's changing awareness of the political-social situation, Ott offers the estimate that it is Bonhoeffer's insistence on the concreteness of life, the inescapability of the situation, which triggers his perception of God's own presence with man, God's presence in Christ. Thus Ott writes of Bonhoeffer's quest:

How can we say to ourselves and to others who Jesus Christ is and how we can find him? In his *Ethics* Bonhoeffer has finally come to this insight and equation, that Jesus Christ equals reality. But this surely implies that he is not only real, that he is not only one reality besides others, *but that he is that reality itself, which or who is the truly real in all that is real.* Wherever we come up against reality, it can be Christ encountering us unawares. *This* is what Jesus Christ is for us. This is the answer to the question about "Who he is!"[35]

Ott's elucidation of the "reality theme" adds a dimension which other interpreters, with the exception of Bethge, had not developed. And of Ott's analysis at this point, Bethge said:

> Ott's focus on the problem of reality as a point of unity in Bonhoeffer's authorship is not inappropriate. . . . I myself have tried to describe the point of unity in all periods in terms of Bonhoeffer's drive toward concreteness but was less successful.[36]

And regarding Ott's work as a whole, Bethge commented: "I should like to maintain that Ott, as no one before him, compels the reader to see the whole of Bonhoeffer's thought."[37]

Analysis of Bonhoeffer's work and exposition of its meaning nevertheless continued, with others attempting to establish ever more precisely the systematic coherence within the developmental pattern of Bonhoeffer's thought. André Dumas, in a 1968 study, offered explication along lines often paralleling those of Ott but sought, in addition, to establish the fundamentally Hegelian character of Bonhoeffer's thinking.[38] Dumas asserts:

> Bonhoeffer's theology was neither transcendental, existential, nor liberal. It can best be described as structural. From his earliest works through the *Ethics,* we find a remarkable continuity in his expression of Christian faith, not as the beyond that is self-authenticating, nor as an encounter that takes place, but as a structuring that combines self-knowledge with self-realization. Before God, Jesus Christ is the center and the responsible structure of reality. He is neither beyond the world nor in the depths of being, but at the center of the empirical world, which is no longer understood pragmatically but as having an ontological structure understood in Christological terms.[39]

Dumas continues with the observation that the categories of "space, logic, physics and geography" are more basic to Bonhoeffer's thought than are those of "time, events, personality, and history."[40] And in this Dumas believes he discerns the influence of Hegel, a Hegel "less concerned to describe the logic of history, or to conceptualize the spirit of an age and a people, than to describe subjective experience in objective terms, in brief, a Hegel who is a logician . . . more than a philosopher of becoming."[41] Despite some reservations about a too-close identification of God and reality in Bonhoeffer's thought, with its concomitant suggestion of pantheism,[42] Dumas hails Bonhoeffer's contribution as a liberating force within contemporary Protestantism:

> But the Protestant tradition has insisted so strongly, with Kant, Kierkegaard, Bultmann and Barth, on God's transcendence over the world, that when Bonhoeffer comes speaking and living God's involvement *in* the world, he sets on fire the thoughts and lives of our generation.[43]

Still other assessments of Bonhoeffer's thought that stress or assume the patterns of continuity could be mentioned and summarized,[44] but such is not necessary to a charting of the main lines of interpretation. Only one further work needs mention and this is Ernst Feil's 1971 study, *Die Theologie Dietrich Bonhoeffers.*[45]

Feil's work is an impressive scholarly analysis and elaborates Bonhoeffer's thought in close conjunction with Bethge's biography of Bonhoeffer. He suggests that the main lines of Bonhoeffer's theology are to be charted in terms of the interrelationship between Bonhoeffer's Christology and his simultaneous awareness and understanding of the world (*Weltverständnis*).[46] According to Feil, Bonhoeffer saw the task of theology as the elaboration of the substance of faith out of the situation of active engagement with the world. Again and again, Feil underlines the point that the form of theology for Bonhoeffer was *a posteriori,* not *a priori.*[47] In Feil's view, Bonhoeffer believed that theology could never state the content of faith once and for all but was itself grounded in discipleship and arose out of concrete historical situations.[48] According to Feil, the empirical church represented to Bonhoeffer a continuing dimension of faith's engagement with the historical situation and—contra Müller and Phillips—was never set aside or lost sight of in the elaboration of a more inclusive Christology. Bonhoeffer's prison letters, for Feil, do not represent an abandonment of ecclesiological concern, but only a deeper, more profound statement of the nature of God's address to the world. Although Feil recognizes a period of theological constriction, or better, "concentration," during the years of the underground seminary at Finkenwalde (*The Cost of Discipleship*),[49] this period of Christological concentration is best understood, in Feil's view, as a call to the church to respond to the concrete message of the gospel.[50] That Bonhoeffer moves beyond the world outlook of *The Cost of Discipleship* is seen not as a disruption of the basic pattern of continuity in Bonhoeffer's thought,[51] but rather as a further development of earlier Christological insights that come into play against the background of an altered situation.[52] Christologically, it is represented as a movement from a concentration upon the "Christ for us" (*pro nobis*) dimension of faith to an affirmation of the "Christ for others" (*pro aliis*), a leading feature of parts of the *Ethics,* but especially of the prison letters.[53] Corresponding to and inseparable from these new Christological accents is a positive, constructive appraisal of the world, expressed in the concepts of the "world come of age" and "religionless Christianity." A concluding aspect of Feil's treatment is his effort to show the systematic coherence of the fragmentary themes of the prison letters and to argue their continuity with Bonhoeffer's "earlier" (1932) theological concerns.

The cumulative effect of the many studies of Bonhoeffer's thought that have been undertaken since the late 1950's has been to establish, almost beyond question, the assumption of substantive continuity in Bonhoeffer's thought. Shifts, new developments, reappraisals are acknowledged, but always the thread of continuity is asserted; and the early thought of Bonhoeffer is seen as a major source for elucidating and lending coherence to the later fragmentary statements of the *Letters and Papers from Prison.* The results, however, of the studies that have pursued the theme of continuity have not been entirely reassuring on this point. As is already apparent in our brief description of the main lines of the new appraisal of Bonhoeffer, efforts to define the thematic unity of Bonhoeffer's thought have not established a consistent picture either of Bonhoeffer's Christology or of the course of his theological development. Only when one moves on into a more thorough analysis and assessment of the issues dividing the major interpretations does the tenuousness of the whole "continuity hypothesis" come into focus.

ᴄᴠᴼ 3 ᴼᴠᴄ

Interpretative
Points of Difference

In taking up an exposition of the most important recent interpretations of Bonhoeffer's thought, one must ask the question whether in the last analysis the differences are not more important than the points of agreement. To be sure, some of the differences can be accounted for in terms of the source materials available to the researchers at the time of their work. Much new material has been made accessible since the late 1950's. The publication in Germany of Bonhoeffer's collected writings[1] and Bethge's exhaustive biography have allowed much greater scope to the investigations of Bonhoeffer's thought. Bethge's biography especially has impressed most later Bonhoeffer scholars with the necessity of taking very seriously the course of Bonhoeffer's life as a crucial dimension of elaborating patterns of his thought. But even with these new source materials, the divergence of interpretation continues and is traceable in four critical areas: in Bonhoeffer's methodology, ecclesiology, Christology, and concern for "reality."

METHODOLOGICAL DIFFERENCES

Gerhard Ebeling early noted some of the methodological problems associated with a study of Bonhoeffer's work. Writing in 1955, before the great wave of interest in Bonhoeffer studies, Ebeling observed:

> In dealing with the person and work of Dietrich Bonhoeffer it is very difficult to resist the tendency to dwell upon the close tie between the theological and the human aspects, as it speaks to us above all in the collection of *Letters and Papers from Prison.* . . . We [are tempted to] . . . speak of Bonhoeffer's theological and spiritual ancestry and his place in the most recent history of theology, of the development he himself underwent, and of his personal life which presents . . . the unforgettable commentary on his theological thinking.[2]

Ebeling suggested that "a comprehensive biography would unquestionably be an eminently important key to the understanding of what he [Bonhoeffer] was commissioned to say,"[3] but Ebeling himself, perhaps for lack of such a biography, opted for a systematic approach: "namely, to renounce all emotional effect and enter on a sober theological examination"[4] of a major subject in Bonhoeffer's later thought, the concept of a "non-religious interpretation of biblical concepts." However, as a basis for his systematic effort, Ebeling arbitrarily presupposed essential continuity between Bonhoeffer's *Ethics* and *Letters and Papers from Prison.*[5] At crucial points in his analysis he refers to statements in *Ethics* as support for his interpretation of Bonhoeffer's later concept, without really establishing the systematic coherence of points of view expressed in *Ethics* with others found in the prison letters. The fragmentary character of Bonhoeffer's thought, not only in *Letters and Papers from Prison,* but also in *Ethics,* allows—even elicits—efforts at "systematic exposition," and these in turn have helped to convey the impression of greater continuity than may in fact exist. That some later interpreters convincingly argued against Ebeling's law-gospel explication of Bonhoeffer's "non-religious interpretation" did not assure greater caution in the tempting leap back and forth between *Ethics* and *Letters and Papers from Prison.* Heinrich Ott, for example, rejects Ebeling's analysis[6] but is himself no less prone to assume continuity between these two volumes. Ott does this on the very questionable grounds that the two works are simply to "be regarded as essentially contemporary."[7] By contrast, Hanfried Müller, though not denying continuity and development in Bonhoeffer's thought, speaks of "qualitative leaps" in his theological development[8] and identifies a final "leap" in Bonhoeffer's movement beyond the thought patterns of *Ethics* to those of *Letters and Papers from Prison.*[9] And another interpreter, Rainer Mayer, again while not wanting to deny a basic continuity in Bonhoeffer's thought, speaks of the collapse of Bonhoeffer's "system of Christological ontology" set forth in *Ethics* as a basis for the transition to the thought patterns of the "world come of age" in the prison letters.[10]

Whereas Ebeling presupposed at crucial points elements of Bonhoeffer's *Ethics* in his analysis of *Letters and Papers from Prison,* Moltmann in his 1959 study made *Ethics* the central focus of his effort to chart lines of continuity running back into Bonhoeffer's earliest writings, *The Communion of Saints* and *Act and Being.* Moltmann deplored the fact that preceding studies of Bonhoeffer's thought (especially Ebeling's) concentrated too much on single ideas in his later writings, with no concern for their basis in underlying themes growing out of his earliest thought. Thus Moltmann sought to correct this pattern by analyzing Bonhoeffer's concept of the "mandates" in *Ethics* against the background of the earlier notions of the "ethical-social transcendence of God," the "entering of God into reality," and "the vicarious action of Christ."[11] Moltmann acknowledged a shift in Bonhoeffer's thinking between *The Cost of Discipleship* and *Ethics,* but insisted that by saying this "we do not mean to imply a breach in Bonhoeffer's work as a whole."[12] Moltmann, while centering his analysis on Bonhoeffer's discussion of the "mandates" in *Ethics,* quotes the prison letters whenever he regards them as helpful in interpreting the "mandates" or illustrative of the underlying themes which he traces from Bonhoeffer's earliest thought. Essentially, however, Moltmann's pattern of systematic analysis is one that moves back and forth between *Ethics* and the earliest writings, of the years 1927–1933, *The Communion of Saints, Act and Being,* and *Creation and Fall.*[13] He does not concern himself with *The Cost of Discipleship*, with the systematic coherence of *Ethics* as such,[14] or with the relationship of *Ethics* to *Letters and Papers from Prison*.

Still another variation in the systematic approach to Bonhoeffer's work is that offered by Heinrich Ott. Like Ebeling and Moltmann, Ott is concerned to construct a picture of ideational coherence, but he is distinctive in establishing extremely flexible guidelines for the definition of this coherence. He insists that the interpreter must recognize at the start the "experimental style" of Bonhoeffer's thought.

> One cannot take every sentence which one reads in Bonhoeffer as there and then his final word, and begin to build upon it a system of thought, or insert it as a finished component into any such systematic reproduction of Bonhoeffer. . . . On the other hand, if one thinks that one has met with contradictions in what he has said, these do not necessarily at once indicate deep discrepancies in his thought as revealed in them. . . . One must be clear on this point, that he experimented in his theological thought, as did many a great thinker before him.[15]

This statement follows immediately upon Ott's assertion of the overall unity of Bonhoeffer's thought. In Ott's words: "The thoughts of his early works remain living and appear again in later contexts in altered form but with unchanged substance. In spite then of all the external lack of unity, a clear inner 'direction' is still typical of his work."[16]

Having insisted on Bonhoeffer's "experimental style" in the context of overall unity—a point of view that makes the delineation of contradictions and shifting foci in Bonhoeffer's thought extremely difficult if not impossible[17]—Ott compounds a tendency toward an eclectic and artificial systematization of Bonhoeffer's thought by asserting a formative role for the interpreter in what Ott defines as a "dialogical" methodology.[18] To be sure, Ott views Bonhoeffer's theological contribution primarily as a "legacy," a legacy that demands refinement and creative elaboration by those who come after; but one has to ask whether Ott's methodology does not allow so much freedom to the interpreter that the givenness of what Bonhoeffer in fact was saying is in danger of being seriously distorted. For example, besides asserting the identity of the present-day interpreter's "situation" with that of Bonhoeffer,[19] Ott suggests that there are certain principles associated with the phenomenology of discussion that provide basic guidelines for interpreting Bonhoeffer's thought. Among the principles are the following: "All statements of our partner in discussion are to be measured and interpreted against what was his last concern. This means that as a rule what he says last is authoritative."[20] Application of this principle means for Ott that "we should understand [Bonhoeffer's] whole work in the light of the theological position which is last to see daylight, that of his *Letters from Prison.*" And Ott goes on to assert: "So far as I know he has recanted nothing of his earlier important statements. What he said later then in *Letters and Papers* and *Ethics,* has a special importance for the interpretation of his whole work."[21] One should note that it is in this context that Ott makes one of his two brief references to *The Cost of Discipleship* and insists on its "teleological interpretation" in terms of *Letters and Papers from Prison* and *Ethics.*

Two other principles operative in Ott's methodology are the idea that discussion "can be creative," with new ideas emerging out of the discussion (in this case, the "discussion" between Bonhoeffer and his interpreter) and the proposal that "because a discussion is not to be understood in itself, but always as an encounter with the subject, it is on occasion legitimate to take a thought out of its context."[22]

It is not surprising that despite his high praise for parts of Ott's work, especially Ott's definition of the "reality" theme, Bethge should seriously question Ott's nearly total neglect of *The Cost of Discipleship.*[23] And Mayer, after a detailed analysis of Ott's methodology, comments: "Ott's dialogical method is his weakness. It bears within it the danger of throwing wide the gates to every mischievous Bonhoeffer interpretation which neither hears him correctly nor properly extends his thinking."[24]

Still another variation in systematic methodology is found in the work of André Dumas, *Dietrich Bonhoeffer, Theologian of Real-*

ity.[25] Unlike other interpreters, who have generally been content to describe two major sources of influence in the shaping of Bonhoeffer's thought (Barth and liberal nineteenth-century Protestant theology), Dumas attempts to fix the thought of Bonhoeffer—and that of twentieth-century Protestant theology as a whole—within the main lines of the philosophical tradition. Dumas's distinctiveness lies in his assertion of major Hegelian influence—in fact, of the *dominance* of Hegelian concerns—throughout the course of Bonhoeffer's theological career.[26] So intent is Dumas on tracing this particular influence that he leaves little room for consideration of other, perhaps more basic, stimuli and concerns.[27] In explanation of his inclusion of a biographical chapter in his book, Dumas says: "After, but only after, having tried to understand this way of thinking, let us now become acquainted with the man. For although the story of a man's life does not create his thought, his life will put it to the test."[28] This way of putting the question suggests that for Dumas the matter of ideational coherence is paramount, a presupposition that governs both Dumas's methodology and his results.[29]

With more or less rigor, Ebeling, Moltmann, Ott, and Dumas[30] pursue methods of systematic analysis that stress the continuity and coherence of ideas in Bonhoeffer's thought over the course of his theological work. One simply does not find in these analyses a serious grappling with discontinuities and shifting emphases in Bonhoeffer's thought, e.g., a discussion of *The Cost of Discipleship* in its relationship to Bonhoeffer's earlier or later writings, the relationship of *Ethics* to *Letters and Papers from Prison,* or the matter of conceptual turning points in Bonhoeffer's work.[31] To be sure, this was not the stated task of Ebeling and Moltmann in their works, but to the degree that they helped to establish the now dominant view of Bonhoeffer's theological work, it is necessary to reappraise their contribution in the light of problems that have increasingly come to the fore *within* this general school of Bonhoeffer interpretation.

Alongside the predominantly "systematic" methods of Bonhoeffer interpretation, what has emerged most recently as a com-

pelling methodological approach is precisely what Ebeling projected years earlier: the attempt to integrate the pattern of Bonhoeffer's thought with the course of his life, to understand his
thinking in relation to the actualities of his personal situation. Here
the work of Bethge has been crucial. In his Chicago lectures of
1961 Bethge discussed Bonhoeffer's theological contribution in
terms of a chronology and periodization that suggested transitional
"moments": "foundation" (1927–1933), "concentration" (1933–
1940), and "liberation" (1940–1945), categories that subsequently
were personalized in the subtitle of the 1967 biography, which
referred to Bonhoeffer as "theologian," "Christian," and contemporary." Bethge's biography has made it virtually impossible for
those arguing for systematic coherence and continuity in Bonhoeffer's thought to ignore any longer the creative stimulus of Bonhoeffer's existential involvements as factors in the shaping of his
thought. This problem, posed in Bethge's biography, was early
noted by Paul Lehmann in a 1967 review of Bethge's work. Lehmann, in connection with Bethge's account of Bonhoeffer's fascination with the Spanish bullfight, points out a "risk": "The risk is,
in part, that those who wish to minimize or disparage the tes-
timonial power of Bonhoeffer's life—and there are not a few, in
Germany and even in the United States, who manage to affect
being unaffected—will find a life of such contrasts and transitions
of sensitivity not so much creatively human as uncreatively confused and unreliable."[32] Lehmann in his review addresses concern
to Bethge at the point of the latter's assertion of a shift in Bonhoeffer's later thinking, a shift dated from April 1944. Lehmann
speaks of this position of Bethge as

> regrettable because it exposes a contradiction in Bethge's interpretation
> of Bonhoeffer. We have already noted that there is less of a gap between
> Bonhoeffer's latest writings and his earliest ones than has hitherto been
> carelessly supposed. Bethge seems at the end to be giving his important
> case away. If there is an organic development in Bonhoeffer's thought,
> why does Bethge admit to a shift? If there is, nevertheless, a shift, what
> is it precisely? Is it a shift of position or of accent? Bethge leaves the
> question unsatisfactorily open.[33]

Lehmann in this question to Bethge raised again the matter of whether essential continuity or discontinuity was the dominant feature of Bonhoeffer's theology, especially in relation to Bonhoeffer's later thinking. One has to ask however whether this is simply a fault in Bethge's interpretation, the suggestion of a "1944 shift," or whether what emerges here is a kind of inevitable concomitant of the whole process of correlating life and thought. At issue here, with the availability of Bonhoeffer's "life" in biographical form, is the question about the dynamics of thought processes in their relationship to the ebb and flow of life itself. It seems increasingly questionable whether the purely "systematic" approach to Bonhoeffer's theological work is adequate, whether grounded in the assumption of an unfolding logic, of some pattern of inner, logical necessity—or even in the form that Moltmann put it when he stated that "the theology of the earlier writings . . . proves their worth when applied to other themes."[34]

In attempting to rectify the deficiencies of the merely systematic approach, others have undertaken studies of Bonhoeffer that might be broadly characterized as "systematic-existential." These studies tend to view Bonhoeffer's thought not as a thing in itself, not simply as an "unfolding," but as a process of interaction between the concerns of faith and the actualities of life—however the latter may be defined.[35]

Certainly the early analysis by Hanfried Müller is of this sort. As Müller describes it, the reality with which Bonhoeffer was conversant was, in major part, social and political in nature. According to Müller, Bonhoeffer's involvements in the social and political realities of his day help to explain the form of Bonhoeffer's theological concerns. While by no means claiming that Bonhoeffer shared a Marxist point of view, Müller finds in Bonhoeffer a growing sensitivity to the realities of the social and political situation. Müller says of Bonhoeffer: "It is notable throughout his entire life that he was able to anticipate with astounding sensitivity the spiritual movements of his time."[36] Müller, following in part Bethge's periodization of Bonhoeffer's life, discerns in each period a responsiveness to social and political conditions that have ever wider ramifications for Bonhoeffer's theology. Thus for Bethge's period of theological "foundation" (1927–1933), Müller asserts that the decline of the Weimar Republic and the crisis of capitalism made crucial the question of real community (cf. *The Communion of Saints, Act and Being*).[37] In the period of the struggle against Fascism (Bethge's period of "concentration," 1933–1940), Müller interprets Bonhoeffer's concern as the need to act within the framework of community (*The Cost of Discipleship, Life Together*).[38] The final period proposed by Bethge, the period of "liberation" (1940–1945), is treated by Müller as two periods, one identified with the work on *Ethics* (1940–1943) in which Bonhoeffer interpreted the struggle against Fascism in the early war years as an effort to preserve "the Christian civilization of the West." Here the "church-oriented ethic" of *The Cost of Discipleship* yields to a "Christian ethic" presupposing the traditional ideal of the *Corpus Christianum* (Christendom).[39] Then, for Müller, a major shift occurs—and this is best interpreted as a fourth period (1944–1945) —when the inevitable defeat of Fascism became apparent after the battle of Stalingrad and B nhoeffer turned to the consideration of an impending new society—a non-Western society, and one that would bear a "non-religious" character. According to Müller, Bonhoeffer's concern in this last period of the *Letters and Papers from Prison* centered around the formulation of an ethic applicable to a simply *human* society and no longer limited to the idea of a "Christian West."[40]

As a partial "corrective" to Müller's interpretation, John A. Phillips, in his 1967 study of Bonhoeffer's theology, argues ambiguously about Bonhoeffer's involvement in events. He says, for example, in criticism of Müller's analysis: "What one wishes to see, however, is sufficient regard for the 'aristocratic' Bonhoeffer who, in Karl Barth's words, 'seemed to move on ahead in another dimension.' Bonhoeffer's *freedom* from time and place and circumstance characterized him beyond all else and astonishes all who read the prison letters. His theology can hardly be summed up as a theology of reaction."[41] And Phillips, at another point, asserts that Bonhoeffer's "theology issued from the tension . . . between unreconciled elements in its Christological centre."[42] This latter statement would seem to describe a systematic methodology on Phillips' part; but, in fact, as Phillips' interpretation unfolds, he lays occasional heavy stress upon historical circumstance as an important factor in Bonhoeffer's theological development. For example, he offers the view that Bonhoeffer's involvement in the Confessing Church's struggle against Hitler inhibited the elaboration of his promising 1933 Christology[43] and also that later restrictions placed upon Bonhoeffer's church activities by the Nazis, along with his participation in the German Resistance movement (after 1939), provided the stimulus for new, progressive ideas found in *Ethics* and the prison letters.[44]

Those studies of Bonhoeffer's thought which come after the publication of Bethge's biography generally reveal major indebtedness to that work and, with the qualified exception of Dumas's analysis,[45] recognize the impact of events upon Bonhoeffer's thought. This is not to say that Bethge's biography has brought or will bring about extensive agreement in fundamental matters of interpretation but only that, methodologically, it has become increasingly difficult to avoid dealing with Bonhoeffer's life experiences as an important dimension of any discussion of his thought.

This point is apparent, for example, in Rainer Mayer's work, *Christuswirklichkeit.* Mayer asserts a major intent by Bonhoeffer to build an ontological system,[46] but goes on to suggest that this effort, culminating in Bonhoeffer's *Ethics,* collapsed, in part at least, as a result both of Bonhoeffer's disillusionment with the Confessing Church and of his experiences in the Resistance movement.[47] Clearly, the building of a "system," especially an ontological system that attempts to delineate a structure of being, sharply inclines one to the logical, systematic task. But Mayer, even though suggesting this to have been a long-term project of Bonhoeffer, insists nonetheless on incorporating into his interpretation the biographical materials and the periodization of Bonhoeffer's life provided by Bethge.[48] The intractability of life—the "world" in Mayer's understanding—called into question Bonhoeffer's systematic formulation and forced reappraisal and new formulation.[49]

Of all who have analyzed Bonhoeffer's work, Ernst Feil gives greatest play to the existential dimension. His interpretation stands at a far remove from Mayer's ontological interpretation, and is even farther removed from Ott's. Feil insists that Bonhoeffer was not in the least interested in building an ontological system,[50] though he argues strongly that there is a continuing and central concern in Bonhoeffer for the problem of theological interpretation. Against Mayer, Feil argues that one must take most seriously Bonhoeffer's argument, in *Act and Being,* against the building of a theological system.[51] Feil works in very close concert with Bethge's biography; and, in addition, he attempts to align his own methodological procedure with Bonhoeffer's understanding of the relation between faith and theology, between *actus directus* and *actus reflexus.* Feil insists that for Bonhoeffer—as for Barth—theology was basically a movement from faith to reason and not vice versa; that God was not to be known *a priori,* though reflection upon faith was necessary.[52] God in his hiddenness, the secret and mystery of God, was not, for Bonhoeffer, accessible to the reason of man, least of all to theoretical, speculative reason.[53] Feil points out that in sharp opposition to the tradition of philosophical idealism, Bonhoeffer stressed actuality over against potentiality; concreteness and thinking-out-of-the-situation over against abstraction. Thus, early in his theological career, Bonhoeffer—in Feil's view—came to perceive that act and deed serve an interpretative, hermeneutical function;[54] and Bonhoeffer increasingly came to find his own place within the context of the church. In contrast to Barth, however, who left the pulpit to become a theologian, Bonhoeffer is presented as one who left the university to become a pastor. Feil sees in what Bethge describes as Bonhoeffer's conversion (1931–1932) and his subsequent abandonment of his university position an essential clue to the pattern of Bonhoeffer's life and thought.[55] The central and provocative point in Feil's methodological discussion is that the interpretative problem confronting an expositor of Bonhoeffer's thought is inseparable from Bonhoeffer's own understanding of theology as grounded in the ebb and flow of the church's life within the world. From this point—and in continuing close liaison with Bethge's biography—Feil moves on to offer an interpretation of the major themes of Christology and Bonhoeffer's understanding of the world.

DIFFERENCES OVER ECCLESIOLOGY

If there are striking differences among interpreters of Bonhoeffer as to how his work is to be approached methodologically, it is not surprising that there also emerge important differences concerning what Bonhoeffer was mainly saying or the direction in which his thought was moving. There are three basic themes that have been identified overall by Bonhoeffer interpreters as constituting cohesive, unifying concerns of Bonhoeffer's theology. These are: ecclesiology, Christology, and the "reality" or "concreteness" theme. The fact of interpretative divergence in the understanding of these themes and disagreement concerning their centrality in Bonhoeffer's thought are points to be especially noted. Great care should be exercised in assessing the meaning and content which these terms bear at different points in Bonhoeffer's life.

Divergence of opinion is certainly apparent in considering treatments of the ecclesiological theme in Bonhoeffer's theology. A majority of interpreters claim a central place for the church in Bonhoeffer's thought, but at least three interpreters raise an important challenge to this view.

Hanfried Müller makes the dropping of an ecclesiological focus in Bonhoeffer's later thought a major point of his analysis.[56] "From the church to the world" is Müller's characterization of the dominant movement of Bonhoeffer's theology as it culminates in the prison letters. Müller underlines Bonhoeffer's growing disenchantment with the church,[57] his recognition, especially in the prison years, of the church's self-serving character.[58] Müller asserts that in a new orientation toward the future, Bonhoeffer envisioned the task of Christians as that of helping to build a new human society, in the course of which they would be called upon to assume the suffering, anonymity, and self-sacrifice of the cross. Müller's point here is that Bonhoeffer's later thought—i.e., *Letters and Papers from Prison* as over against *Ethics* and the earlier writings—is characterized by the elimination of a *theologia gloriae* (a triumphant Christ and church) in favor of a *theologia crucis* (a humiliated Christ and church).[59] In Müller's view, Bonhoeffer anticipated a declericalization and desecularization of the church, one that would involve the surrender of all status and privilege. This would call for the abandonment by the church of all outwardness, all visibility, though a place would remain for a "secret discipline" in the lives of Christians. All this, Müller feels, was an aspect of Bonhoeffer's "non-religious interpretation" of the Biblical message in the midst of a "world come of age."[60]

Similar to Müller's treatment of Bonhoeffer's ecclesiology is that of John Phillips. Phillips does not, like Müller, view Bonhoeffer as projecting the virtual dissolution of the visible church. Rather, he suggests that in *Letters and Papers from Prison* ecclesiology had become a "side issue."[61] Phillips declares: "Up to the beginning of the *Ethics* in 1940 the church was the central theme in his thinking. But there follows an unmistakable break with this pattern."[62] Phillips points to the fact that in the original prison correspondence between Bonhoeffer and Bethge, Bethge had, at a very early stage in the discussion of Bonhoeffer's new turn of thought, raised the question whether any room was left for the church.[63] It was a question that was never satisfactorily answered. In Bonhoeffer's letter of June 8, 1944, the question was noted: "Now for your question whether there is any 'ground' left for the church, or whether that ground has gone for good." No answer was given. Instead, there was a concluding note, dated June 9: "I'm breaking off here, and will write more tomorrow."[64] Phillips comments on this: "Tomorrow did not come, and Bonhoeffer's vision remains incomplete. Should we complete the picture by pointing towards Bonhoeffer's previous interest in a doctrine of the church?"[65] Phillips does *not* argue, as does Müller, that ecclesiology virtually disappears in the forms of a new human society. "We have enough clues (though they are no more than clues)," Phillips says, "to know that Bonhoeffer wanted to discuss the role of the church in the area of the 'secret discipline,' and that he regarded this as the dialectical partner and corrective of 'religionlessness.' "[66] But the point is forcefully made by Phillips that ecclesiology cannot be regarded as a major expression of continuity in Bonhoeffer's thinking.[67]

Rainer Mayer also lends support to this judgment, when, in describing the breakdown of Bonhoeffer's ontological system (between *Ethics* and *Letters and Papers from Prison*), he asserts that the concept of the concrete, visible church was the first casualty of that collapse and that Bonhoeffer thereafter revealingly introduced a new term into the fragmentary discussions about the church, that of "unconscious Christianity."[68]

DIFFERENCES OVER CHRISTOLOGY

Disagreement among Bonhoeffer's most positive interpreters over whether or not ecclesiology represents a unifying theme in his thinking is probably not a decisive matter. This is so despite the fact that for some interpreters a very close relationship exists between ecclesiology and Christology—a point especially true of Godsey.[69] However, with regard to Christology itself, the issue is quite different because all of the major interpreters mentioned in our survey agree on the basic Christological focus of Bonhoeffer's work, even when this is considered in conjunction with some other theme such as ecclesiology, or the varying interpretations of the "reality" motif. It is asserted that from the doctoral dissertation *The Communion of Saints* (1927) through to the *Letters and Papers from Prison* (1943–1945), Bonhoeffer's basic focus of thought was Christology.[70] Yet, when one considers the substance of these expositions of Bonhoeffer's Christology no greater agreement is found on this point than in the other areas of methodology or ecclesiology.

Ebeling's early monograph did not have an analysis of Christology as a major purpose, but Moltmann cites the concept of "deputyship" as a fundamental unifying theme in Bonhoeffer's overall thought. He suggests that deputyship is "a strictly christological doctrine."[71] In elaborating this concept of "deputyship" in relation to the question of social ethics, Moltmann links it with the idea of vicarious representation and asserts that this idea underlies Bonhoeffer's "theology of society."[72] Moltmann points out that in *The Communion of Saints* Bonhoeffer had said: "The unique quality of the Christian idea of acting vicariously is that this action is strictly vicarious with regard to guilt and punishment. Jesus, being himself innocent, takes the others' guilt and punishment upon himself, and as he dies as a criminal, he is accursed for he bears the sins of the world and is punished for them; but on the felon's cross, vicarious love triumphs; obedience to God triumphs over guilt, and thereby guilt is in fact punished and overcome."[73] Moltmann comments concerning this passage: "In *Ethics* and in his last letters from his prison cell at Tegel, Bonhoeffer could call this vicarious action 'Being for others' (Christ the man who lives for others)."[74] It is Moltmann's contention that "deputyship," a major theme of a section of the *Ethics*,[75] is identical with the idea of vicarious representation in *The Communion of Saints* even though, in *Ethics,* Bonhoeffer's "horizons are broadened to include the Lordship of Christ not only in the church, but also in the world."[76] Moltmann declares: "Bonhoeffer takes up the Christology and ecclesiology of vicarious representation which he had worked out in *The Communion of Saints* and develops it further in *Ethics,* applying it to all life created and redeemed by Christ for human fellowship under the mandates of the world."[77] Moving beyond *Ethics,* Moltmann asserts that this is also the context and content of Bonhoeffer's enigmatic statement in *Letters and Papers from Prison:* "Before God and with God we live without God. God lets himself be pushed out of the world on to the cross. He is weak and powerless in the world, and that is precisely the way, the only way, in which he is with us and helps us. Matt. 8.17 makes it quite clear that Christ helps us, not by virtue of his omnipotence, but by virtue of his weakness and suffering."[78]

Whereas Moltmann accents vicarious representation and insists on its continuous expression throughout Bonhoeffer's writings, Hanfried Müller claims to see in Bonhoeffer a movement away from a Christology of exaltation (*theologia gloriae*) to a Christology of the cross (*theologia crucis*). As already noted, Müller asserts a sharp demarcation between *Ethics* and *Letters and Papers from Prison*. Although he allows that dimensions of Bonhoeffer's later thought may have been anticipated at points in his earlier writings, he suggests that they were generally bound up with impeding emphases and were thereby restricted in scope. However, in the spring of 1944, according to Müller, these ideas broke forth into a fuller development in conjunction with Bonhoeffer's anticipation of the collapse of Fascism and his adoption of a new, more positive orientation toward the world.[79] Bonhoeffer thereupon abandoned every effort to establish a manifest lordship of Christ (or a lordship for the church) over the world and turned to a renewed stress upon the hiddenness of God in his revelation. Müller writes:

> It is simply a matter of acknowledging that it pleased God to oppose in weakness the godlike strength of sinful man, that precisely this is God's grace. Because man in his sin is not weak but strong, and because God in his grace is not strong but weak, therefore Bonhoeffer is concerned *not* to confront man in his weakness with an omnipotent God. That means that the Last Judgment is not to be anticipated, that this-worldliness is not to be prematurely surrendered, . . . that the grace of God, which is grounded in God's weakness and suffering, is not to be turned aside for the sake of the majesty of God, a majesty before which man can only perish. Bonhoeffer is concerned rather that the strong, mature man meet God in his suffering in the world, which is, in this life, the hidden strength of God.[80]

According to Müller, standing behind all of Bonhoeffer's later thought, even though not explicitly stated, is Luther's dialectic of the revelation and the hiddenness of God and also of the wrath and the grace of God. "It is God's grace," writes Müller, "that in his suffering and death we may believe in his majesty and power without having now to view it in mortal Judgment."[81] Thus Müller in the end finds in Bonhoeffer a kenotic Christology, one that emphasizes the surrender by God of all ruling attributes in the assumption of the human form of Christ. It is in this form that God is "*for* all men."[82]

With John Phillips, as previously noted, still another interpretation of Bonhoeffer's Christology is offered. Phillips asserts that there are essentially two conflicting Christologies in the thought of Bonhoeffer. One charts a restricted sphere of Christ's lordship and is found in Bonhoeffer's earliest writings, *The Communion of Saints* and *Act and Being,* and also in *The Cost of Discipleship.* Phillips argues that in these writings Christology is closely bound up with ecclesiology,[83] and the church is set over against the world. However, a second, more encompassing Christology ascribes universal scope to Christ's lordship. According to Phillips, this second Christology is to be found in Bonhoeffer's 1933 Christology lectures at the University of Berlin and also in Bonhoeffer's later writings, *Ethics* and *Letters and Papers from Prison.*[84] This more universal Christology, in Phillips' view, is forced into the background over the course of the German church struggle (1933–1939), but emerges again with Bonhoeffer's involvement in the conspiracy against Hitler and the elimination of many of the parochial concerns of the Confessing Church.[85] While noting that some themes from the earlier Christology are carried over—e.g., the humiliated form of the Christ, the hiddenness of revelation, Christ's work on behalf of man (*pro me*)—Phillips insists that with the second Christology "Bonhoeffer has moved beyond the limitation of 'Christ existing as the church' to a conception of the person of Christ as both the center and boundary of the individual believer. He has located the central Christological problem not in the relationship of God to Jesus nor of Jesus to the church, but in the manner in which Jesus is in the world, for others."[86] At another point Phillips writes:

> For *The Cost of Discipleship,* transcendence means primarily freedom from the world. . . . This "breach with the world," made relevant and concrete in the issues of the church struggle, characterized this phase of Bonhoeffer's life and thought. . . . But in the prison letters, the "boundaries" which delineated this breach with the world have disappeared. It is not merely coincidental that Bonhoeffer's interest in ecclesiology disappeared at the same time. What remains is the interest in the participation of the disciple in the transcendent being of Christ. There is, of course, a major alteration: in *The Cost of Discipleship,* being *for* the world in Christ could only mean separation *from* the world. The

prison letters neatly reverse this, following the meditation on the "worldliness" of Christ which begins in the *Ethics:* freedom from the world can only be spoken of as the participation in Christ's *being-for-others.*[87]

Arguments defining a shift in Bonhoeffer's Christology as expressed by Müller or Phillips—themselves not in agreement on the nature of the shift—are emphatically rejected by Ott. Ott insists on the essential continuity of Bonhoeffer's thought from beginning to end. As grounds for this he places heavy emphasis upon an autobiographical reflection in Bonhoeffer's *Letters and Papers from Prison.* Bonhoeffer's makes the statement: "I don't think I have ever changed very much, except perhaps at the time of my first impressions abroad and under the first conscious influence of Father's personality. It was then that I turned from phraseology to reality. . . ."[88] Ott comments on this: "The 'turn from phraseology to reality' was for him from the beginning bound up with the name of Jesus Christ, and the *motif* of the Christological structure of all that is real is a note already sounded in, for instance, his doctoral dissertation. . . ."[89] Ott argues: "This view of Christ as the truly real upholding all reality is maintained throughout his work, it may be with varying nuances, but without any material break."[90] It is present, he asserts, in Bonhoeffer's 1933 lectures on Christology,[91] but most explicitly in the *Ethics.* Ott elaborates:

In the *Ethics,* which essentially is contemporary with his prison letters, the thought of a Christological ontology, which already appears in his earlier works, has found its most crucial form. To make clear what we are saying about "Christological ontology," let us bring forward the text which Bonhoeffer quotes at the one decisive point. Col. 1:16 runs (N.E.B.), "In him (sc. Christ) everything in heaven and on earth was created." . . . and v. 17 continues, "and he exists before everything, and all things are held together in him." It is this universalist trend in the New Testament witness to Christ which Bonhoeffer is seeking to follow in his thought of a Christology to be developed ontologically. And the Christ who is so experienced and so thought of is no longer the religiously "transcendent" Christ or the Jesus of the individual soul." He is the Christ in all reality.[92]

Ott asserts: "In his *Ethics* Bonhoeffer has finally come to this insight and equation, that Jesus Christ equals reality. But this surely implies that he is not only real, that he is not only one reality besides others, but that he is that reality itself, which or who is the truly real in all that is real."[93] Ott's subsequent elaboration of this Christological reality centers in the assertion of a personalism that represents the climax or summation of reality. Addressing himself to the theme of "conformation" found in the *Ethics,* Ott declares: "Jesus is present as the essential form of man, the form of the incarnate God to whom we are conformed. Conformation presupposes his form as a *prius.* Jesus Christ himself, in person, is the primary reality, to which the man who exists ethically surrenders himself in order so to become truly 'real.' "[94] In this grounding of personhood, Christ is "the center of human existence," "the center of history," and also "the center of nature."[95]

Such an ontological interpretation of Bonhoeffer's Christology is endorsed also by Dumas, who declares: "I think Ott has correctly grasped Bonhoeffer's central purpose, which was to understand and follow the structuring presence of God in reality by means of the Christology of the incarnation and to overcome the dualism of metaphysics and inwardness by an ontology of presence and openness."[96] In his own discussion of Bonhoeffer's Christology, however, Dumas not unexpectedly presses his thesis of major Hegelian influence in a chapter entitled "Jesus Christ as Structure and Place."[97] Dumas here devotes the entirety of his discussion to an exposition of Bonhoeffer's 1933 Christology lectures and a 1933 lecture on "The Nature of the Church." As justification for this procedure Dumas says:

> It is better not to end with *Letters and Papers from Prison,* as though the whole of Bonhoeffer's thought were summed up in those final flashes of insight from his prison cell. The continuity of his thought is too apparent as can be shown by the stability of his vocabulary. Words like reality (*Wirklichkeit*), deputyship (*Stellvertretung*), and structuring (*Gestaltung*), for example, ran through all his works, and nowhere are they more clearly defined than in the texts of 1932–33.[98]

Dumas stresses the role of structure and place in Bonhoeffer's 1933 lectures, asserting: "Bonhoeffer speaks of Jesus Christ both as a place and as a structure of the world around us and almost never refers to him as an event in history."[99] For Dumas, "Christology is not only that portion of theology devoted to the study of redemption. It is also the description of what can give meaning to the word 'God' as well as the word 'reality,' since the work of Jesus Christ consists in making each evident to the other in the unified relationship that reveals them both."[100] While allowing that for "religiously inclined people" the Christ event, a past historical event, can be made the bearer of special "meaning" and "emotion," Dumas insists that Christology "in addition"—and more properly—"will now claim to interpret the fundamental structuring of what is, thus becoming the interpretive center of theology, ontology, anthropology and cosmology."[101]

Dumas's ontological interpretation of Bonhoeffer's thought was published one year before Rainer Mayer's analysis (1969) and thus neither writer—unfortunately—had the benefit of the other's insight. It is to be noted that even within this school of ontological interpretation the two works of Dumas and Mayer reflect major differences in viewpoint. Mayer, it will be recalled,[102] suggests that there is an important cleavage between the *Ethics* and the *Letters and Papers from Prison,* which he describes as a collapse of Bonhoeffer's efforts in the *Ethics* to construct an "ontological system." This "collapse" is defined as Bonhoeffer's abandonment of the attempt to view all of reality through the person of Christ,[103] but it does not, for Mayer, represent an abandonment of what was always fundamental for Bonhoeffer, the reality of Christ (*Christuswirklichkeit*). This "reality of Christ" is spelled out by Mayer chiefly in relation to Bonhoeffer's two earliest writings, *The Communion of Saints* and *Act and Being.* It is Mayer's contention that Bonhoeffer's teacher, Reinhold Seeberg, posed the dogmatic question with which Bonhoeffer basically wrestled over the years, the question "How can God's involvement in the world (revelation) be described without at the same time abridging His supramundane character (transcendence)?"[104] Bonhoeffer, according to Mayer, re-

jected Seeberg's own proposed answer framed in terms of "the pure
spirituality of God's will" in favor of a Christocentric approach in
which he shared common ground with Karl Barth.[105] Commenting
on the relationship of Bonhoeffer to Barth, Mayer declares that
with both men "revelation encounters us only in Christ. Christology is the point of departure for which there can be no prior
grounding and from which all else must be derived. Human structures are merely integrated into the Christological totality as clari-
fying elements. But for this reason Bonhoeffer—now in distinction
from Barth—is concerned that this also really happens: i.e., that
the immanent world is visibly laid hold of and transformed by
revelation. That must be shown!"[106]

The ontological dimensions of Mayer's analysis are most clearly
expressed in terms of the categories of "act" and "being," the
former bearing the content of "transcendence" and the latter bearing that of "immanence" and continuity. In *Act and Being*, Mayer
suggests, Bonhoeffer explored the *philosophical* dimensions of the
concept of revelation, which he had initially treated in terms of
sociological categories in *The Communion of Saints*. He points out
that Bonhoeffer regarded the tension between a theology of being
and a theology of act as a major motif of the long tradition of
theology and credited both alternatives with a positive content.
The theology of being, according to Bonhoeffer, was classically
represented through Thomism; the theology of act was represented
through the contemporary "dialectical theology." Mayer suggests
that Bonhoeffer's "solution" to the one-sidedness of either alternative was to argue for the "act-being unity" of the church, a phrase
applicable also to the person of Christ.[107] Both in the reality of
Christ and in the church there is a blend of transcendence and
immanence. The individual is confronted in Christ by a new sense
of personhood in which the other, the "Thou," no longer encounters the individual merely as "an ethical limit," but in which,
rather, "God in Christ reveals his love . . . as self-giving 'I', opening
his heart [to man]."[108] Christ, however, is not only individual but
also collective person; and through his death and resurrection, a

supratemporal and supraspatial significance is established. Both Christ and the church bear a cosmic character.[109] In a manner recalling Moltmann's analysis of the movement of Bonhoeffer's thought,[110] Mayer asserts that this Christological formulation develops out and away from the "ecclesiastical concentration" of the early writings in the direction of "Christocratic breadth."[111] And, according to Mayer, when we find Bonhoeffer confronted with the collapse of his attempts to formulate an ontological system in the *Ethics,* this is not to be viewed as an abrogation of his basic ontological Christology in its "act-being unity."[112]

As a final example of Christological interpretation, one must cite again the views of Ernst Feil. In sharp opposition to the efforts to interpret Bonhoeffer's Christology in ontological terms, Feil argues that there is little if any trace of this ontological interest after the 1933 Christology lectures, and that in fact, in *The Cost of Discipleship,* there is "a warning against the confusion of ontological assertions with proclaiming witness."[113] Feil concurs in the judgment of another scholar, J. M. Meier, that in Bonhoeffer's work as a whole there is lacking a "specific concept of being"[114]— a point of view that clearly contradicts the positions of Ott, Dumas, and Mayer.

Feil's own point of departure in the treatment of Bonhoeffer's Christology is related to his methodological argument about the importance of Bonhoeffer's life situation and the precedence of the *actus directus* over the *actus reflexus.*[115] It is in relation to *Act and Being* (1931) and implicitly in conjunction with Bethge's assertion of some kind of conversion experience in the years 1931–1932 that Feil discerns in Bonhoeffer a clearly defined Christological concern, even though this was anticipated somewhat in Bonhoeffer's 1928 Barcelona lectures and sermons. Contrary to most previous interpreters, Feil finds a lack of Christological focus in *The Communion of Saints.*[116] This earliest work of Bonhoeffer is regarded by Feil as a first scholarly endeavor, "ecclesiocentric" in argument and weak in its understanding of history.[117] With *Act and Being,* however, and in Bonhoeffer's 1931 Union Theological Seminary lectures, Feil believes Bonhoeffer laid a firm grasp on the contingency of revelation as a historical event and thereafter sharpened his Christological focus.[118] From this point, according to Feil, Bonhoeffer moved on to affirm Christ as both the "Center" and the "Boundary" of human existence (*Creation and Fall*, 1932/1933). and also as the "Mediator" (Christology lectures, 1933).[119] Here Christ's lordship was viewed as extending over existence, history, and nature,[120] leading Feil to argue that a concern for the world was clearly present at this point and that this concern carried through the period of the church struggle, manifesting itself even in Bonhoeffer's *The Cost of Discipleship.*[121] In the course of his exposition Feil takes pains to point out what he feels to be the inadequacies of Phillips' account of the development of Bonhoeffer's Christological thought, asserting that the middle period of Bonhoeffer's work does *not* involve a withdrawal to the earlier ecclesiology of *The Communion of Saints* or a loss of world outlook.[122] Rather, this middle period is best understood, says Feil, as a Christological deepening of earlier views, a deepening that finds expression in the displacement of all immediacy by Christ.[123] This mediatorial role for Christ is then further elaborated and expanded in the incomplete *Ethics,* with its projection of a Christocentric understanding of the world. Feil asserts that Bonhoeffer found in Christ reinforcement for an increasingly positive understanding of, and turning toward, the world. Not through God or some understanding of creation independent of Christ, but rather through Christ himself Bonhoeffer is brought to a positive world-understanding in full accord with the classical Chalcedonian formulation.[124] The importance of history and historical existence, though never neglected from the time of *Act and Being* on, is strongly reasserted as a crucial dimension of "worldliness" and attack is made on an otherworldly eschatology that would deprive both the world and history of their God-given meaning. Feil asserts that Bonhoeffer's concern for the world and the affirmation of historical existence carries through *Ethics* with the categories of the "penultimate" and "ultimate," to the *Letters and Papers from Prison,* in which "Bonhoeffer concerned himself above all with the inner-worldly future, with the 'afterwards' of the time which was to follow the [Nazi] catastrophe."[125] In this context Feil insists that Bonhoeffer in no way encouraged a criticism of God's transcendence but rather endeavored to interpret God's transcendence as nearness. Bonhoeffer did this, Feil suggests, through a new probing of Christology expressed in the question: "Who is Christ for us today?"[126] According to Feil, his new probing of Christology, though bearing the marks of the classical Lutheran themes of the condescension and hiddenness of God,[127] is not to be understood as the isolation of a "theology of the cross" and its separation from a "theology of exaltation" (contra Hanfried Müller).[128] Rather, it is best understood as a shifting of accent from the significance of Christ "for me" or "for us" to the meaning of Christ "for others."[129]

DIFFERENCES OVER CONCRETENESS, REALITY, WORLDLINESS

A third theme found in the writings of Bonhoeffer and cited by some of his interpreters as a unifying theme of his theology is the concern for "concreteness," sometimes also identified as the theme of "reality" or of "worldliness." Though by no means as central or well defined as the Christological emphasis—a point on which all of his most positive interpreters are agreed—this concern of Bonhoeffer for "concretion" in the Christian faith, a concern that faith meet face-to-face the realities of the world, is purportedly traceable throughout the course of Bonhoeffer's written work.

In *Act and Being* Bonhoeffer, in criticism of Barth's "formalistic understanding of God's freedom," asserted:

> In revelation it is a question less of God's freedom on the far side from us, i.e., his eternal isolation and aseity, than of his forth-proceeding, his *given* Word, his bond in which he has bound himself, of his freedom as it is most strongly attested in his having freely bound himself to historical man, having placed himself at man's disposal. God is not free *of* man but *for* man. Christ is the Word of his freedom. God *is there,* which is to say: not in eternal non-objectivity but . . . "haveable,"

graspable in his Word within the Church. Here a substantial comes to
supplant the formal understanding of God's freedom.[130]

And again in a letter to a friend in 1931, Bonhoeffer wrote: "How
do you conceive of the imperishableness of Christianity in view of
the world situation and our own manner of life? . . . Who still
believes that? The invisibility destroys us. . . . This continually
being thrown back upon the invisible God himself—that no man
can any longer endure."[131]

In his Chicago lectures of 1961, Bethge made this motif of
"concreteness" the subject of his opening discussion of Bonhoeffer's thought. He made two points in this connection: first, that
for Bonhoeffer concreteness was an "attribute of revelation itself,"
and secondly, that the message of the church to the world had also
to be concrete. In regard to the first point, Bethge asserted that in
the early writings and continuing throughout the later, "Incarnation is . . . at the heart of Bonhoeffer's theology. There cannot be
any speculation about a God before or outside this concreteness.
The incarnated God is the only one we know. We cannot even
think of concreteness as an addition God put on later to his being.
All we know, and this is breathtaking, is that the incarnated concreteness is *the* attribute as far as we can think."[132] Bethge continued: "Here it becomes obvious how much Bonhoeffer develops
his Lutheran heritage, as he presents his case in criticizing Barth's
neo-Kantian transcendentalism—God the *ganz andere,* the nega-
tion of all we know and do. Bonhoeffer fully accepted and saw the
great contribution of Barth in the uncompromising emphasis on
the contingency of revelation, so that it might never become an
object for our handling. . . . But this interest Bonhoeffer sees
safeguarded not in the beyond but in the Christ 'existing as the
community of men.' "[133] Bethge suggests that the issue here between Bonhoeffer and Barth is a continuation of the classic issue
between Lutheranism and Calvinism, with Bonhoeffer asserting
the Lutheran point of view that the finite is capable of bearing the
infinite (*finitum capax infiniti*) versus the Barthian, Calvinistic

position that the finite is not capable of bearing the infinite (*finitum incapax infiniti*).[134]

The concern for concretion that finds expression in Bonhoeffer's early statements about revelation, ecclesiology, and Christology carries over, according to Bethge, into Bonhoeffer's later emphasis on the church's address to the world and ethics. Here, "only the message which becomes a specific concrete word is the eternal word of authority."[135] Concreteness is to be known not only within the life of the church but also in the church's proclamation. Bethge notes: "In an ecumenical conference paper in 1932 [Bonhoeffer] says that the concreteness of the gospel is present and safeguarded in the sacraments—but where is the specific sacramental concreteness of God's commandment? He answers: 'What the sacrament is for the proclamation of the gospel, the knowledge of concrete reality is for the proclamation of the commandment. Reality [*Wirklichkeit*] is the sacrament of the commandment.' "[136]

According to Bethge, Bonhoeffer's concern for concreteness is found not only in the earlier works but in *The Cost of Discipleship,* where it finds expression in the relationship between the believer and Christ. Again, the concreteness motif finds expression in the *Ethics,* where Christ's lordship over the world is manifested in the specifics of the "mandates" through which social, economic, and political life are ordered and structured. Bethge concludes by saying that "concreteness is still not the aim or the result of the explorer on his tour; it is in Bonhoeffer's sense always the presupposed equipment for the tour, which waits with surprising discoveries. The real concreteness derives from grasping the essential concreteness of Christ."[137]

Some years later (1967), in reviewing Heinrich Ott's *Reality and Faith,* Bethge praised Ott's treatment of the "reality theme" and declared it to be a step beyond his own discussion of Bonhoeffer's drive toward concreteness.[138] Bethge's deference to Ott's more comprehensive discussion is interesting but should not be interpreted to mean that Bethge simply acquiesced in Ott's analysis. In fact Bethge, in this same review of Ott's book, raised serious questions about Ott's Christological interpretation, suggesting that he had failed to do justice to Bonhoeffer's "theology of the cross"—a criticism that carries wide implications, since it touches not only upon the question of Christology, but upon the question of reality as well. In this regard, Bethge observed: "Ott does not sufficiently guard his universalistic-ontological concerns from the danger that the claim of the gospel on the world will eventuate in a resacralization and a new clericalization of the world. Hanfried Müller is sensitive to this danger and reacts . . . whenever 'reality' is 'integrated' on the basis of ontological Christology . . . , when all reality 'is determined' through Christ . . . , or when the 'structures' of reality are preserved through him."[139]

What is at issue here is Ott's propensity for an ontological personalism. In contrast to other interpreters who see Bonhoeffer as wrestling with an ever-changing "concrete world," or who conceive of Bonhoeffer's "reality" as an understanding of history, Ott defines Bonhoeffer's "reality" as essentially the experience of personal encounter—an experience, it should be noted, that is not restricted to the believing community or the consciousness of faith.[140] Ott interprets Bonhoeffer as saying that

> as Mediator, as Reconciler between God and man, Christ is the true reality and . . . every other understanding of reality apart from him is an abstraction. This does not of course mean that there could be no other reality from a Christ . . . , but rather that all that is real is sustained as the real by the reality of this One. . . . The components of the event of Christ, for Bonhoeffer the Incarnation, Cross and Resurrection, are the final ontological components of all that is reality at all. . . . The reality which we experience is in all its complexity, differentiation, and incomprehensibility permeated and determined by Christ. . . . [Christ] is something in himself, as a person. He himself creates through himself a universal reality, the reality of God and man, the reality of the world reconciled by God, accepted by God and indwelt by God, the reality of the grace before the face of God in which man and world always already stand. This reality is a sphere of encounter.[141]

Accordingly, Ott accents very strongly Bonhoeffer's early probings of the nature of Christian community, "Christ existing as a community," and what he feels to be its later form in the *Letters and Papers from Prison*, the assertion that Jesus' " 'being-there-for-others' is the experience of transcendence." Ott makes central the words of Bonhoeffer: "The transcendental is not infinite and unattainable tasks, but the neighbor who is within reach in any given situation, God in human form."[142]

It is important to note that Ott's personalistic reading of "reality" allows little if any room for Bonhoeffer's attempts at an interpretation of history. These efforts are especially prominent in *Ethics*, where Bonhoeffer offers an analysis of the heritage of the Christian West, and in the *Letters and Papers from Prison*, where account is given of "man's coming-of-age."[143] Ott, in opposition to Hanfried Müller, argues that these historical analyses by Bonhoeffer are "little thought over and scarcely worked out."[144] Ott rejects out of hand Müller's contention that the differences between these two interpretations of history signalize Bonhoeffer's breakthrough into a new understanding of and openness toward social and political "reality" (i.e., a semi-Marxist understanding of history).

The divergent views of Ott and Müller on the question of Bonhoeffer's understanding of "reality" can hardly be reconciled, since Ott proposes an ontological personalism, whereas Müller insists on viewing Bonhoeffer's work against the background of a Marxist interpretation of history. However, even when one moves away from interpretative extremes, as it were, differences in viewpoint are no less striking. For example, even between Dumas and Ott, both of whom affirm an ontological interpretation of Bonhoeffer's thought, major disagreements are to be discerned in their separate descriptions of Bonhoeffer's view of "reality." Dumas shares with Ott the tendency to deemphasize Bonhoeffer's historical analyses; but in stating his own thesis, Dumas also diminishes the significance of personalistic categories essential to Ott's interpretation. In assessing Bonhoeffer's theme of concretion, Dumas insists that spatial and geographical categories are determinative over against those of "time, events, personality, and history."[145] Dumas offers a description of Bonhoeffer's "spatial" definition of "the concrete":

"He discovered it first of all in the empirical state church that refused, for conservative reasons, to succumb to the temptation of perfectionist separatism. As a young man, Bonhoeffer was a defender of 'Christendom' in a way that was most disconcerting to his later readers. In *Ethics,* he was still trying to preserve the heritage of the 'Christian west.' He next embodied this emphasis on the concrete in relation to the Confessing Church making a specific decision in its favor the crucial test of truth in the midst of reality, both in Nazi Germany and in the ecumenical movement."[146] And moving on to the last phase of Bonhoeffer's thought (*Letters and Papers from Prison*), Dumas speculates about the meaning of Bonhoeffer's phrase "anonymous Christianity" and concludes that it could *not* signify simply "a church of silence and waiting." Such a conception would, Dumas contends, come much too close to that "duality between the visible and the invisible church, between idea and fact, between God and reality, against which Bonhoeffer never stopped fighting."[147] Dumas asks rhetorically: "Without concretizing the church, how could there be a concrete commandment, and furthermore how could there be a real coming to grips with the concrete world? Naturally, the church must do battle against 'religious' evasion, provincialism and shortsightedness, on behalf of the incarnation and the fullness of the faith in the midst of reality, but how can this be done concretely, if the church does not have a 'place' and a concrete embodiment?"[148]

Final illustration of the lack of agreement among interpreters of Bonhoeffer's view of "reality" is afforded again by Feil, who not only rejects an ontological interpretation of Bonhoeffer's thought as a whole but insists on the primacy of the very historical and personalistic-existentialist categories that Dumas rejects. As already indicated, Feil views Bonhoeffer's theology primarily as an outgrowth of faith's involvement in the historical process. Not only is God's personhood best understood in terms of the freedom to act, but theology's task is to mirror that engagement of God with the world which is epitomized in the incarnation. With Feil the content of the terms "reality" and "concrete" is spelled out in the description of the interrelationship of Christology and "world-understanding." And Feil offers the conclusion that Bonhoeffer's Christological concerns were increasingly related to a shifting, developing world-understanding that grew out of Bonhoeffer's own faithful, experiential engagement with life.[149] By 1939, Feil argues, Bonhoeffer made explicit the bond between Christology and world-understanding, and this in a very positive sense.[150] Between 1939 (*Ethics*) and 1944 (*Letters and Papers from Prison*) however, Feil notes that a significant reappraisal of the nature of the world (i.e., history) takes place, and that this reappraisal was articulated through Bonhoeffer's 1943–1944 studies of the writings of Wilhelm Dilthey. Clearly Feil comes close to confirming aspects of Müller's analysis in identifying an important shift in Bonhoeffer's historical understanding between the *Ethics* and the prison letters. But Feil holds back from—and in fact rejects—Müller's description of this turn of thought as a "qualitative leap," a sort of break with previous patterns of thought.[151]

Feil's impressive documentation of Bonhoeffer's conceptual dependence on Dilthey for the later image of a "world come of age"[152] represents a major contribution to our understanding of the origin of some of Bonhoeffer's later ideas. Feil argues, however, that despite the dependence upon Dilthey, Bonhoeffer's originality as a thinker is still to be seen in his rejection of Dilthey's concept of religion and his conviction that the maturity and autonomy of modern man offer Christian faith the chance to become real in a new and more profound way.[153] In this connection, Feil comments: "One will not be able to say that Bonhoeffer simply bound up the revelational theological impulse of Karl Barth with the world-understanding of liberal theology, but rather that Bonhoeffer, through Karl Barth's theology, conceived a Christian world-understanding that neither gave in to the world at the cost of faith nor for the sake of Jesus Christ overlooked the world."[154] All things considered, what Feil basically asserts is that in the prison letters, the concept of "reality" and that which had then become "concrete" for Bonhoeffer, was an image of "the autonomy of the world" as set forth in the historical (*geistesgeschichtliche*) analyses of Wilhelm Dilthey and as confirmed by Bonhoeffer's own experiences.[155]

To be sure, with this survey we have *not* exhausted all the analyses that argue for the major theological significance of Dietrich Bonhoeffer and that also, in the process, assert a basic theological continuity in Bonhoeffer's intellectual development. But, in the opinion of the present writer, the most important of these studies have been outlined in their main arguments and it remains now to offer an assessment of these scholarly endeavors and ask if the case for Bonhoeffer's coherent and increasingly perceptive theological development has in fact been made. In my view this case has not been made and room must still be allowed for the earlier assertion of Bonhoeffer's impulsiveness and visionary tendencies. An explanation of, or way of viewing, this "impulsiveness" will be offered in a later chapter. But first a further discussion of the conflicting points of view among Bonhoeffer's interpreters must be undertaken. The impression must not be given that these interpretations all have equal worth.

~ 4 ~

Assessment
of Points at Issue

The foregoing survey of the major points at issue among the more positive interpreters of Bonhoeffer's theological contribution suggests that no clear consensus has thus far emerged in regard to the developmental lines of Bonhoeffer's thought. What is striking about the variety of interpretations offered is that each interpreter is able to marshal arguments of weight and cite passages in Bonhoeffer's writings that lend credence to the particular interpretation being offered. Müller, for example, is able to quote in a surprisingly effective manner a variety of passages from Bonhoeffer's writings to support his semi-Marxist interpretation. Ott does the same for his ontological personalism, Dumas for his Hegelian analysis, Mayer for his "act-being unity" and so forth. Most frequently it is material omitted or ignored in the analysis that is most damaging to the case being made.

It may well be that in the years ahead Feil's analysis will mark the beginning of some sort of scholarly consensus regarding the central focus and thrust, if any, of Bonhoeffer's thought, but even Feil's work is open to challenge at crucial points. Certainly Feil's interpretative endeavor is methodologically the most competent and persuasive—a judgment no doubt open to question, but difficult nonetheless to avoid. As previously noted, Feil's work is the most comprehensive in treating other interpretations and in identifying strengths and weaknesses in the preceding interpretations. His use of Bethge's biography and his integration of it into his exposition of Bonhoeffer's thought, his awareness of, and openness to, the question about breaches and turning points in Bonhoeffer's theological development, his scope in dealing with all of Bonhoeffer's major and minor works: these features make Feil's interpretation noteworthy. He is able to hold in effective restraint the systematic tendency to ignore situational involvements and to equate superficially similar ideas within Bonhoeffer's early and later thought.[1] That is to say, one finds in Feil an openness to allowing personal and historical realities to find their place in the exposition of what Bonhoeffer was saying at different times and in different periods of his all too brief theological career.[2] This is not to say that Feil abandons the common supposition that binds most of the present studies of Bonhoeffer together, i.e., the assumption of an underlying unity to Bonhoeffer's life and thought.[3] But Feil insists that this underlying unity must be viewed in the context of Bonhoeffer's life and not independently of it. Like many others, Feil cites the autobiographical reflection of Bonhoeffer that is found in the prison letter of April 22, 1944. In that letter Bonhoeffer observed:

> When you say that my time here will be very important for my practical work, and that you're very much looking forward to what I shall have to tell you later, and to what I've written, you mustn't indulge in any illusions about me. I've certainly learnt a great deal, but I don't think I have changed very much. There are people who change, and others who can hardly change at all. I don't think I've ever changed very much, except perhaps at the time of my first impressions abroad and under the first conscious influence of father's personality. It was then that I turned from phraseology to reality. I don't think, in fact, that you yourself have changed much. Self-development is, of course, a different matter. Neither of us has really had a break in our lives. Of course, we have deliberately broken with a good deal, but that again is something quite different. Even our present experiences probably don't represent a break in the passive sense. I sometimes used to long for something of the kind, but today I think differently about it. Conti-

nuity with one's own past is a great gift, too. . . . I'm often surprised
how little (in contrast to nearly all the others here) I grub among my
past mistakes and think how different one thing or another would be
today if I had acted differently in the past; it doesn't worry me at all.
Everything seems to have taken its natural course, and to be determined necessarily and straightforwardly by a higher providence.[4]

Feil refers also to Bonhoeffer's statement about the fragmentary
character of life for people of his generation and underlines Bonhoeffer's expressed hope that "we should be able to discern from
the fragment of our life how the whole was arranged and planned,
and what material it consists of."[5] Feil contends, consistent with
the main thrust of his interpretation, that it is the unity of Bonhoeffer's life that provides the foundation for understanding the
continuity of Bonhoeffer's thought.

But here, despite the instructive and provocative aspects of
Feil's analysis, one must consider other, contradictory statements
that Bonhoeffer makes about the course of his life and thought. For
example, one must note that the April 22, 1944, letter quoted above
does *not* give support to the very important contention of Bethge
and Feil that Bonhoeffer "the theologian" became "the Christian"
sometime during the years 1931–1932. Bonhoeffer cites only his
father and his first trips abroad as formative influences, or turning
points, in his life. Also, in a 1932 letter to a friend, Erwin Sutz,
Bonhoeffer remarks that Sutz has found too much good in his book
Act and Being and that "in the meantime I have come rather to
dislike the work"[6]—this despite Feil's rather convincing argument
that an explicit Christological focus emerges in *Act and Being*
whereas such is not present in *The Communion of Saints.* Further,
one is simultaneously puzzled and illumined by Bonhoeffer's retrospective reflection in prison that earlier "I thought I could
acquire faith by trying to live a holy life, or something like it. I
suppose I wrote *The Cost of Discipleship* as the end of that path.
Today I can see the dangers of that book, though I still stand by
what I wrote."[7] And again, there is the question of how properly
to assess Bonhoeffer's statement to Bethge in the important letter
of April 30, 1944: "You would be surprised, and perhaps even

worried, by my theological thoughts and the conclusions that they lead to"[8]—or the passage in the baptismal message (May 1944): "Reconciliation and redemption, regeneration and the Holy Spirit, love of our enemies, cross and resurrection, life in Christ and Christian discipleship—all these things are so difficult and so remote that we hardly venture any more to speak of them. In the traditional words and acts we suspect that there may be something quite new and revolutionary, though we cannot as yet grasp or express it."[9]

It is, of course, true, as Feil points out, that in his letters Bonhoeffer gave unguarded expression to many thoughts and ideas that certainly would not have been expressed as they were in a formal theological work. Thus a certain discretion and caution is enjoined in assessing some of these utterances.[10] Nevertheless, it is the case that Bonhoeffer's own descriptions of his life and theological development are ambiguous at best. And some of his later concepts and phrases are sufficiently puzzling (e.g., "non-religious interpretation of biblical concepts," "revelational positivism," "secret discipline") to call forth speculative attempts to reconstruct the wellsprings and main flow of his thought. Here it is noteworthy, as already indicated, that a variety of interpretations seems in fact to be possible, all bearing a degree of plausibility.[11] What is impressive about Feil's methodological approach is his unwillingness to embrace speculative reconstruction at the cost of what he feels to be the vital features of Bonhoeffer's life. Feil accents Bonhoeffer's early "leap of faith" (1931–1932) and argues that this plays the formative role in the *a posteriori* character of his theology. Feil attempts to establish his interpretation of Bonhoeffer's subordination of the *actus reflexus* (speculative theology) to the *actus directus* (the immediacy of faith within the framework of the church)[12] by means of an excursus in which he describes Bonhoeffer's abandonment of a secure future in the academic world for the uncertainties of the church and a pastoral role, leading on to his ever-deepening involvement in the church struggle against Hitler and finally to his participation in the plot against Hitler's life.[13] It is, however, unfortunate that Feil did not choose to pursue this same methodological procedure at another crucial turning point in Bonhoeffer's theology, that represented by the shift of thought between the *Ethics* and the later prison letters and signalized by his "discovery" of Dilthey. Instead, Feil is strangely insistent that Bonhoeffer's later reflections concerning a "world come of age" and the "non-religious" character of modern man "are grounded *not biographically* in Bonhoeffer's personal development, but *historically* in a profound change of the times."[14] Feil suggests, rather incongruously in the light of his major argument, that at the point of his affirmation of the "world come of age" Bonhoeffer had attained an objective, disinterested perspective on the world's "historical situation" and that he was not there inspired by any special personal considerations or experiences. At this point, it would seem, Feil's methodological procedures may have come under some systematic constraint. But it will remain for our discussion in the following chapter to try to establish this point.

THE ECCLESIOLOGICAL THEME

If Feil bids well to offer the beginnings of a helpful and provocative methodological approach to the exposition of Bonhoeffer's thought, this should not be interpreted as an acquiescence in most of Feil's conclusions. Certainly partial agreement on the methodological question limits, in some measure, the interpretative possibilities that attend Bonhoeffer research. But even within the limits of an existential-systematic approach to Bonhoeffer's thought there are still many ways of viewing and assessing the interplay of life and thought that is so much a part of the Bonhoeffer legacy.

On the matter of the place of ecclesiology in Bonhoeffer's theology, for example, Feil represents something of a mediating position between the views of Müller and Phillips on the one hand and John Godsey on the other, the latter insisting on a close and unbroken tie, both early and late, between Christology and ecclesiology.[15] Feil breaks with Godsey in calling into question the Christological character of Bonhoeffer's earliest work, *The Communion of Saints,* a work that Feil considers essentially church-centered but ambiguous and unclear on the question of revelation as a historical event.[16] Thus, for Feil, Bonhoeffer's Christological focus first emerges in *Act and Being,* the 1931 Union Theological Seminary materials, and the Christology lectures of 1933. On the other hand, Feil rejects the suggestion of Müller that ecclesiology basically fades from view in the prison letters—or is reduced to the level of a "side-issue," as Phillips would have it.[17] Feil regards both church and sacraments as a continuing concern of Bonhoeffer through even the prison letters, though he argues that the theme of world-understanding and its dialectical correlation with Christology is most basic.[18] With Bethge, Feil believes that the "secret discipline" of which Bonhoeffer speaks in the prison letters is properly to be understood as an indication of a continuing, important role for the church; but he goes on to suggest that for the later Bonhoeffer the world is better first confronted by the authentic deed of the Christian than by "the Christian message and above all [by] the Christian service of worship in baptism, communion, and confession."[19] Feil asserts: "That certainly does not mean that there are now two types of preaching, one for the [Christian] community and one for the world, but rather that the service of worship of the community does not belong on the street."[20] And at another place he says, "It is to be maintained that Bonhoeffer's non-religious Christianity may *not* be understood as the elimination of cult, sacrament, sermon, and prayer; that love of God and love of neighbor may *not* be identified; that the 'Christian thing to do' is not the same thing as the 'ethical' . . . ; rather, the tension of the ultimate and the penultimate, the polyphony and the multidimensionality (of life), must be held onto to the end. Then alone is [a] profound this-worldliness substantiated and preserved as 'genuine worldliness.' "[21]

However sensible Feil's views at this point appear to be, and however inclined one may be to agree with him that Bonhoeffer was not consciously about the business of conflating faith and "worldliness," if one nevertheless isolates out of the whole corpus of Bonhoeffer materials his attitude toward and understanding of the church, one is very much impressed with the fluctuations in his ecclesiological interests and conceptualizations. One therefore seems hardly justified in proposing ecclesiology as a unifying and formative theme in Bonhoeffer's theology as a whole.

For example, one notes Bonhoeffer's early sensitivity to the question of community and what he then projects—perhaps somewhat idealistically—as the nature of Christian community in *The Communion of Saints.*[22] Yet one is not convinced that this early conceptualization held up long under the hard realities of the church struggle and Bonhoeffer's own personal struggle for faith. In *The Communion of Saints,* Bonhoeffer quite clearly sided with the personalistic rebellion against philosophical idealism, an intellectual feature of the post–World War I era; and he there reflected the influence of Eberhard Grisebach along with that of Friedrich Gogarten, Reinhold Seeberg, and more indirectly that of Ferdinand Ebner and Martin Buber.[23] Bonhoeffer's own early embrace of confessionalism in the church struggle and his attraction to the "free church" idea is difficult to reconcile with the personalistic ecclesiology found in *The Communion of Saints.*[24]

Even more noteworthy is Bonhoeffer's later, very great dependence upon Kierkegaard in the formulation of the thought of *The Cost of Discipleship.* In *The Communion of Saints,* Bonhoeffer shows only a limited familiarity with Kierkegaard's thought:[25] he supports Kierkegaard's attack on idealism, but then strongly rejects Kierkegaard's individualism as an expression of that same idealism.[26] Later, however, and in the context both of the church struggle and what Bonhoeffer defined as the period of his own struggle for faith (to be arrived at by means of living "a holy life"), Bonhoeffer's much more careful reading of Kierkegaard resulted in the striking adoption of many of the concepts and terms of the Danish existentialist. The similarity of Bonhoeffer's thought in *The Cost of Discipleship* with Kierkegaard's has been superficially noted by some other interpreters such as Woelfel[27] and Dumas.[28] But one Kierkegaard researcher, T. Vogel—cited by Bethge and Feil[29]—has shown that in fact a great deal of the actual terminology of *The Cost of Discipleship* has a Kierkegaardian origin. The contrast between "faith" and "doctrine," the terms "immediacy" and "reflection," "worldliness" as life "without discipleship," the "extraordinary," the significance of the "situation" for faith, "either/or," the proper understanding of "cloister," and the term "discipleship" itself are all identifiable as Kierkegaardian borrowings. Vogel's research indicates that these borrowings came not from a general reading of Kierkegaard but from an anthology of Kierkegaard materials compiled by W. Kutemeyer and published in 1934 under the title *Der Einzelne und die Kirche* ("The Individual and the Church"). Bethge has confirmed these conclusions of Vogel and indicated that Bonhoeffer's own heavily underlined copy of Kutemeyer is still in existence.

One notes this development in Bonhoeffer research because it very much calls into question the idea of progressive development, at least in Bonhoeffer's ecclesiology. Feil, for example, wonders at some of Bonhoeffer's strongly "individualistic" expressions in *The Cost of Discipleship* and suggests further that perhaps something of Bonhoeffer's limited view of "worldliness" during this period was the result of the powerful, temporary influence of Kierkegaard.[30] What one has here is a pattern not unsimilar to Bonhoeffer's already noted "Dilthey discovery," which underlies the "world come of age" image in the prison letters. In both instances Bonhoeffer moves from an intellectual ethos that is essentially post–Kierkegaard (the personalism of Grisebach, Gogarten, Buber) and post–Dilthey (the neo-orthodox critique of the Enlightenment) to champion a position generally regarded to have been theologically superseded. In both cases one must entertain the possibility that these "reversals" are perhaps more related to patterns of Bonhoeffer's own personal development and personal exigency—a point to be argued more fully in the ensuing chapter—than they are to the processes of intellectual growth and increasing social-historical awareness.

Efforts have, of course, been made to resolve this Kierkegaardian "detour" and assimilate it once again into the mainstream of Bonhoeffer's thought. Thus Dumas proposes that *Life Together* (1939) should be viewed as Bonhoeffer's own corrective to the individualistic tendency in *The Cost of Discipleship,* and he offers the comment: *"The Cost of Discipleship* called for the creation of a church of disciples. It demanded saints. In describing the church as it is experienced by the disciples, *Life Together* put human beings back into it."[31] Dumas further asserts: "Bonhoeffer speaks [in *Life Together*] of community life as a gift of grace, that moment of repose 'among roses and lilies, of which Luther speaks,' but to which Kierkegaard scarcely refers in his *Edifying Discourses* for the individual."[32] Yet Dumas not once offers a comparison of *Life Together* with some of the impressive statements of corporate life that are to be found in *The Communion of Saints.* To have done so would perhaps have suggested that Bonhoeffer's ecclesiology, or descriptions of corporateness, in *Life Together* are still governed by the watchword "discipline," the theme of *The Cost of Discipleship.* Despite some very moving and realistic observations about community in *Life Together*[33] there are also passages that surprise one in the reading—for example, Bonhoeffer's high praise of and demand for unison singing within the Christian congregation. Bonhoeffer writes: "There are some destroyers of unison singing in the fellowship that must be rigorously eliminated. There is no place in the service of worship where vanity and bad taste can so intrude as in the singing. . . . Unison singing, difficult as it is, is less of a musical than a spiritual matter. Only where everybody in the group is disposed to an attitude of worship and discipline can unison singing, even though it may lack much musically, give us the joy which is peculiar to it alone."[34]

The striking unevenness of Bonhoeffer's statements about the church and communal life in *Life Together* and elsewhere suggests that ecclesiology is more the subject of adjustment to other more dominant concerns than it is a unifying theme itself. Such a judgment becomes even more compelling in the light of the later writings, in connection with which Müller, for example, traces the turn away from the church to the world, and where, as Phillips points out, both Bonhoeffer and Bethge, in the original prison correspondence, indicate that the nature and form of the church had become problematical.[35]

Instructive also, in the light of Feil's major emphasis upon the distinction between the *actus directus* and the *actus reflexus* is the radically altered thrust of this distinction in the later writings from what it was in the earlier. In the 1930 lecture on "Man in Contemporary Philosophy and Theology," the *actus directus* was expressive of a nonreflective, active involvement in the life of the church, the prior ground of all valid theology,[36] whereas in the prison letter of July 27, 1944, a variation of the thought is mentioned in connection with an "unconscious Christianity," an extraecclesiastical, nonconfessional form of faith.[37]

Very clearly, ecclesiology plays no formative role in Bonhoeffer's later thought. And, although it may be rather surely asserted that the Bonhoeffer of the prison letters intended no abandonment of the church, one can hardly look to ecclesiology as a constitutive, unifying theme in his thought as a whole.

THE CHRISTOLOGICAL THEME

On the matter of Christology and the question of *its* formative role in Bonhoeffer's theology, judgments are more difficult to make because the evidence is more complex. It certainly appears that over the major part of his theological career, Bonhoeffer attempted to order his thought "Christocentrically." After *The Communion of Saints,* as Feil points out, Bonhoeffer no longer contemplated a knowledge of God independent of Christ but held to the fully contingent and historical character of God's revelation in Christ.[38] Subsequently he stressed the mediatorial role of Christ in his 1933 Christology lectures, in *The Cost of Discipleship,* and also in sections of *Ethics.* And even with his embrace of a "world come of age" Bonhoeffer tried to focus on the meaning of Christ and what this implied in a newly defined autonomous world. Thus, on the matter of a Christ-centered concern, there appears to be little question: Bonhoeffer was consistent in his probing of the meaning of Christ and he sought to know that meaning for himself and for others.

But having said this we have by no means said all. The problems of Christology are manifold. And we have not satisfied all the questions that are to be asked about the patterns of Bonhoeffer's thought simply by uttering the words "Christology" or "Christocentrism." Here the legacy of Barth is a large one. The theological world has generally taken to heart the insistence of Barth that Christology lies at the very center of Christian theology. But some caution must be exercised here. "Christocentrism" has, it appears, frequently been equated with Christology; and this is a rather dubious equation. For, though a man's thought may be characterized by a Christ-centered concern, this does not, of itself, assure the presence of a well-defined Christology. One can, for example, be a forthright exponent of a "Christocentric" doctrine of revelation and yet not go on to develop a consistent Christology. Also, one can be Christocentric in a quest: one can pursue both in life and thought the meaning of faith in Christ without really arriving at a precise Christological formulation. That is to say, as the exposition of the meaning of the person and work of Christ, Christology is not merely a Christ-oriented doctrine of revelation; nor is it simply the personal quest for the meaning of Christ. Both can lead on to a Christology, but in themselves they are not Christology. Especially, in distinction from a quest, Christology presupposes a meaning already known; it is, as Feil reminds us, *a posteriori* reflection and not speculative projection. These distinctions are important to keep in mind in assessing the varied assertions made by most of Bonhoeffer's interpreters—those who have claimed to find in Bonhoeffer's Christology the unifying center of his thought.

It has already been pointed out in the survey of points of difference among Bonhoeffer's interpreters that great disparity of viewpoint exists in the area of Christological interpretation. This disparity is sufficient of itself to raise a serious question about the claim made for Christology's controlling function in Bonhoeffer's thought. If, in fact, Christology *does* play such a role, why is there not more agreement among interpreters on the nature of that Christology? It is certain that the varied interpretations of Bonhoeffer's Christology cannot all be right. Ott, Dumas, and Mayer all claim that Bonhoeffer arrived at an ontological Christology early in his theological career and spent the remainder of the short time that was his working out the implications of this Christology amid the involvements of the church struggle and the later conspiracy. Ott's proffered interpretation is that of an ontology of personalism, Dumas's that of a "Hegelian" structuralism, and Mayer's that of the balance between transcendence and immanence ("act-being unity"). No agreement exists even among these representatives of an "ontological" persuasion; each presents a picture of the development of Bonhoeffer's thought at variance with the others' views.

Then, alongside the ontologists there are those who describe a movement in Bonhoeffer's Christological thought, a movement from one Christology to another. Thus, Phillips describes a shift in Bonhoeffer from an ecclesiocentric to a world-embracing Christology, one that makes room also for the individual's relationship to Christ. Godsey and Moltmann see a consistent Christology, framed in classical terms, but given ever wider scope in Bonhoeffer's later thought. Müller describes Bonhoeffer's movement away from a theology of triumphalism (*theologia gloriae*), accenting Christ's (and the church's) manifest lordship, to a theology of humiliation (*theologia crucis*), accenting the hiddenness of God and Christ's suffering in the world. And, finally, Feil points to a movement in Bonhoeffer's thought from an emphasis on the meaning of Christ "for me" to the meaning of Christ "for others," insisting that this movement represents a process of deepening insight but not a rejection of earlier patterns.

It is clear that many of Feil's arguments against some of the earlier Bonhoeffer interpretations are well taken. He discounts attempts at an ontological interpretation by pointing to the absence of a doctrine of being in Bonhoeffer's thought and underlining also Bonhoeffer's very early rejection of "system."[39] He also raises questions for those who trace continuity in Bonhoeffer's Christology back to *The Communion of Saints* (this includes Moltmann, Godsey, and Phillips in some degree); he argues that an authentic Christology emerges only with Bonhoeffer's 1930–1931 assimilation of the contingency of revelation in history (i.e., *Act and Being* and his Union Theological Seminary lectures and papers).[40] He does not find the uniqueness in Bonhoeffer's 1933 Christology lectures that both Phillips and Dumas acclaim,[41] nor does he accept the contention of Phillips and Müller that *The Cost of Discipleship* is theologically and Christologically a backwater, cut off from the main flow of Bonhoeffer's thought.[42]

Yet questions remain—and are raised—even by Feil's analysis. Here the distinction between Christocentrism and Christology has an important bearing on the matter. For what Feil does not explain in connection with his denial of the Christological character of *The Communion of Saints* is the nature of Bonhoeffer's concern in that earliest work and how it came about that Bonhoeffer soon declared a distance also from *Act and Being* in his 1932 correspondence with Erwin Sutz.[43] It would seem that Feil's contention of a marked transition from *The Communion of Saints* to *Act and Being* is overstated and that there is operative in Bonhoeffer's subsequent dissatisfaction with *Act and Being* a factor inadequately dealt with by Feil, and by Bethge—the matter of Bonhoeffer's personal and continuing quest for faith.

In regard to *The Communion of Saints,* what Bonhoeffer seemed to be most concerned with in that discussion is not so much Christology—as Feil rightly observes—as the reality of revelation over against the philosophical traditions of empiricism and idealism.[44] Bonhoeffer, in concert with an existentialist personalism (the "I-Thou" motif),[45] declared for the actuality of revelation in the sociological form of the church. Bonhoeffer especially struck out against idealism in attempting to make room for the concrete reality of revelation;[46] and later, in further discussion, he uses the term "Christ" as a synonym for revelation. "There can be no thought," Bonhoeffer writes, "of a second incarnation of Christ (say, in an individual man), but rather we must think of a revelatory form in which 'Christ exists as the church.' "[47] And, when Christological discussion, properly speaking, *does* take place, Bonhoeffer uses it to buttress his basic argument that the church is equivalent to *Christus praesens* (i.e., Christ's presence), which in turn is equivalent to revelation.[48] In an assessment of the main lines of Bonhoeffer's thought in *The Communion of Saints* it seems fair to say that, despite a brief discussion of Christ's vicarious sacrifice and its implications for life in community, basically the major theme is an ecclesiological interpretation of revelation rather than a Christocentric one.[49]

With *Act and Being* there occurs the transposition of the question of revelation from a sociological to a philosophical frame of reference. The subject of concern is essentially the same, though the thought is definitely more Christocentric. The strong polemical attack against empiricism and idealism is continued but is also supplemented by an attack on all autonomous philosophy (especially that of Heidegger). Bonhoeffer's basic orientation toward a transcendent, yet concrete, revelation is clear.[50] The definition of this revelation is now however reinforced by the assertion of the contingency, the event-character of God's self-disclosure in Christ.[51] There is a major appreciation for history and eschatology in *Act and Being,* yet there is also a carry-over of concern for the ecclesiological form of revelation. Bonhoeffer writes:

> Revelation, then, happens within the communion; it demands primarily a Christian sociology of its own. The distinction between thinking of revelation individualistically and thinking of it in relation to community is fundamental.[52]

Though one can concede Feil's point about a sharpening of focus upon Christ in *Act and Being,* the main thrust of Bonhoeffer's argument continues the polemic against idealism and individualism. If one is in search of Christological exposition, however, one finds it here only in a limited way; and it is not surprising that when Bonhoeffer was working on his Christology lectures in 1932–1933 he should describe them as "the most difficult" he ever prepared.[53] The fact of this stated difficulty makes understandable the formal and rather stylized character of these lectures.

Still utilizing existentialist, personalistic categories Bonhoeffer, in the Christology lectures, states once again the limitations of reflective thinking, offering criticism of idealism and philosophy generally, and defining faith in terms of the *actus directus,* the immediate relationship between the believer and Christ. Along these lines Bonhoeffer insists that Christology begins with the *Christus pro me,* the present Christ known in "Word," "Sacrament," and "Community." Only subsequently in his lectures did he move on to the "historical Christ" of the Biblical record or a treatment of the classical Christological statements of Christian history. Basic to his overall discussion is the distinction between the question "Who?" and the question "How?" Since for Bonhoeffer the latter is indicative of objectifying thought and negates the *actus directus,* [54] an attempt is made to develop a Christology of the person of Christ in his humiliated and exalted being, but leaving out of discussion the whole of the Christological tradition having to do with the atonement (the work of Christ). It is not surprising that in the light of this artificial simplification ("who"/ "how") so little should be said in these lectures of vicarious sacrifice. [55] Jaroslav Pelikan's very critical judgments about Bonhoeffer's Christology lectures, his question about the adequacy of the "who"/"how" delineation as a framework for Christological discussion, and his disappointment with Bonhoeffer's scholarly range, seem not unwarranted. [56]

Something that seems, above all, to be increasingly operative at this stage of Bonhoeffer's Christological thought and that helps to explain some of the turns of his later thinking, is the interplay both of a logic of revelation and a personal quest for the meaning of faith. The logic of revelation is Bonhoeffer's increasingly comprehensive grasp of the Barthian attack upon natural theology, idealism, and theological rationalism. In the years immediately after World War I, Barth, Gogarten, Bultmann, and others—following Kierkegaard—challenged every prior rationalistic ground for the understanding of revelation and simultaneously asserted the freedom and transcendence of God. Interpreting the historical catastrophe of World War I as a radical challenge to the assumption of the omnicompetence of "reason," dialectical theology reasserted the authority of Scripture and the "otherness" of the Word of God. Very early in his own theological career Bonhoeffer was caught up by this point of view and, despite some acute criticisms of aspects of Barth's thought in his earliest writings, [57] became an increasingly articulate spokesman for theological confessionalism as an alternative to theological rationalism. Emphasis on I-Thou relationships, the hiddenness of God, the contingency of revelation in historical event, the centering of all revelation in Christ, the event-character of the Word of God: these motifs of dialectical theology are also constitutive building blocks in Bonhoeffer's pattern of thought. Bonhoeffer, in fact, made his own contributions to this "logic" of dialectical theology with his idea of the analogy of relationship in the little essay *Creation and Fall* (1933) and also with his later Christocentric interpretation of the mandates set forth in *Ethics*. But Bonhoeffer's personal quest for faith was a troubled and anxious one during these same years, and served as a complicating factor in his theological development. The quest for faith introduced uncertainty into aspects of Bonhoeffer's Christology and helps to explain some of the unexpected turns in his thinking.

Here, in asserting the importance of Bonhoeffer's quest for faith, one is forced to take issue with a major point in Eberhard Bethge's interpretation of Bonhoeffer's life. Bethge's contention that sometime in 1931–1932 "the theologian" became "the Christian" is not convincing in the light of Bonhoeffer's later explicit statement that *The Cost of Discipleship* was the end of a phase in which he tried to "acquire faith by trying to live a holy life."[58] All the materials that Bethge cites in relation to Bonhoeffer's so-called "conversion"[59] can be as effectively read—indeed, *more* effectively—as part of an ongoing "quest" rather than an "arrival." For example, much, much more of what follows in Bonhoeffer's life and writings can be fitted into an understandable pattern if room is left for the continuation of this quest and the uncertainties attending it. Bonhoeffer, in the same prison letter (July 21, 1944) in which he identified the underlying motivation of *The Cost of Discipleship*, stated that his subsequent alternative to "trying to live a holy life" was to learn to have faith by "living completely in this world."[60]

Up through *The Cost of Discipleship, Life Together,* and even a major portion of the *Ethics,* there was a mutually reinforcing relationship between the Christocentric logic of Bonhoeffer's theology (essentially, dialectic or "Barthian") and Bonhoeffer's personal quest, earnestly pursued amid the harsh realities of the historical situation. Bonhoeffer's theological and personal concern was clearly Christ-centered, but the Christology itself was uncertain and ambiguous; for Bonhoeffer seemed to have been seeking an "encounter with the Christ," the *actus directus*. This quest moved on from the Christ of Word, Sacrament, and Community in the Christology lectures to the One who calls the disciple and demands obedience in *The Cost of Discipleship*.[61] It is not surprising that a discovery of Kierkegaard followed upon the gradual disenchantment with the ecclesiastical possibility of faith—a possibility that was exhausted in the struggle against the pro-Nazi "German Christians" and in disappointment with the indecisiveness of the "ecumenical church." The corporate aspect of *Life Together*, drawing upon the experiences of the Finkenwalde experiment, only partially "corrected" the more individualistic thrust of *The Cost of Discipleship*.[62] But the pattern of corporate discipline in *Life Together*, including the structured efforts at meditation and confession, while no doubt part of Bonhoeffer's personal quest, did not really establish itself as a corporate experience.[63]

In the matter of Christology, *The Cost of Discipleship* places major emphasis on the imitation of Christ, in spite of Bonhoeffer's effort to balance this with the theme of justification by faith. The attempt to hold the two themes together is expressed in Bonhoeffer's oft-quoted phrase: "Only he who believes is obedient, and only he who is obedient believes."[64] But "faith," Bonhoeffer asserted, "only becomes faith in the act of obedience."[65] And, over against a Protestant tendency to transform the good news of the gospel into "cheap grace," Bonhoeffer insisted upon "costly grace," which meant not only "obedience" but "suffering." He wrote:

> An abstract Christology, a doctrinal system, a general religious knowledge on the subject of grace or on the forgiveness of sins, render discipleship superfluous, and in fact they positively exclude any idea of discipleship whatever, and are essentially inimical to the whole conception of following Christ. With an abstract idea it is possible to enter into

a relation of formal knowledge, to become enthusiastic about it, and perhaps even to put it into practice; but it can never be followed in personal obedience. Christianity without the living Christ is inevitably Christianity without discipleship, and Christianity without discipleship is always Christianity without Christ.[66]

Commenting on a passage from Luke's Gospel (Luke 9:57–62), Bonhoeffer declared: "[Jesus] shows the would-be disciple what life with him involves. We hear the words of One who is on his way to the cross, whose whole life is summed up in the Apostles' Creed by the word 'suffered.' "[67] And Bonhoeffer further observed: "Jesus is a rejected Messiah. . . . Suffering and rejection sum up the whole cross of Jesus. To die on the cross means to die despised and rejected of men. Suffering and rejection are laid upon Jesus as a divine necessity. . . . Jesus must therefore make it clear beyond all doubt that the 'must' of suffering applies to his disciples no less than to himself."[68] He then summarized the nature of discipleship in the following terms: "Discipleship means adherence to the person of Jesus, and therefore submission to the law of Christ which is the law of the cross."[69]

Despite efforts to allay concern that the definition of "costly grace" might be interpreted as a call *simply* to the imitation of Christ and an invitation to human achievement,[70] despite the reassertion in a final section of the corporate context of the Christian life[71] and the statement about being "conformed" to the image of Christ,[72] Bonhoeffer's major point is made in connection with his definition of discipleship and the charge that "the word of cheap grace has been the ruin of more Christians than any commandment of works."[73] In point of fact one is confronted in *The Cost of Discipleship* with a kind of Christological mélange, reflective, I think, of Bonhoeffer's own uncertainty about the *Christus pro me.* Besides the *imitatio Christi,*[74] one finds anticipations of the cosmocratic Christ of the *Ethics* in Bonhoeffer's contention that Christ displaces all of the world's immediacies,[75] a motif derived from the logic of revelation rather than from the fulfillment of Bonhoeffer's quest. There are suggestions also of a kind of regal Christology, similar to the cosmocratic, but accenting the absolute authority of

Jesus to command obedience and to call people to discipleship.[76] And again, there are suggestions of the idea of substitutionary atonement.[77]

To be sure, this picture of varied Christological statement can be viewed as an expression of the many dimensions of meaning that have been, and can be, found in the Christ event, a reflection of the fact that no single Christology achieved dominance either on the pages of the New Testament or in the history of Christian doctrine. On the other hand—and in the light of Bonhoeffer's own retrospective statement of what he was about in *The Cost of Discipleship*—one can, as suggested, also view the variety of Christological expression as a symptom of uncertainty arising out of Bonhoeffer's own personal quest.[78] The question of the meaning of the *Christus pro me* had really not been settled and the quest was still in progress.

Of significant note in the continuation of the search for meaning is the striking shift in the assessment of the world that takes place between 1937 (*The Cost of Discipleship*) and 1940 (*Ethics*). Whereas "the world" was essentially a negative term in Bonhoeffer's call to discipleship and demanded separation or conquest,[79] or was preserved by God simply for the sake of the faithful,[80] in the *Ethics* the world increasingly becomes Christ's own realm and Christ is understood to be Christ only in the midst of the world.[81] To the degree that the Barthian logic of a transcendent revelation manifest in Christ still held sway—and this certainly is evidenced in the *Ethics*—there lingers on a polemical thrust in Bonhoeffer's thought that denies a "good" outside of Christ,[82] that views conscience, independent of Christ, as a refuge for human self-righteousness,[83] and that interprets the last two centuries of Western history as having fallen under the sway of an alien, self-destructive spirit.[84] But more importantly, there is in *Ethics* the significant shifting of ground that then becomes most apparent in the *Letters and Papers from Prison,* the bold affirmation of the world and man's coming-of-age as the basis for asking, "Who is Christ for us today?" In *The Cost of Discipleship* the very essence of discipleship was a break with the world and the recognition of the "extraordinary,"[85] but in *Ethics* there is apparent an increasingly positive assessment of the world. In the former work the operative logic was "outside the church there is no salvation,"[86] but in the section of the *Ethics* entitled "The Church and the World"[87] a sort of rapprochement with the world is under way. Here the church's role in the preservation of culture is asserted and Bonhoeffer argues that increasingly those who struggle for the general values of Western culture are finding a nearness to Christ. The passage that describes this movement in Bonhoeffer's thought is important and deserves full quotation:

> Reason, culture, humanity, tolerance and self-determination, all these concepts which until very recently had served as battle slogans against the church, against Christianity, against Jesus Christ Himself, had now, suddenly and surprisingly, come very near indeed to the Christian standpoint. This took place at a time when everything Christian was more closely hemmed in than ever before and when the cardinal principles of Christian belief were displayed in their hardest and most uncompromising form, in a form which could give the greatest offence to all reason, culture, humanity and tolerance. And indeed it was precisely in inverse proportion to this narrowing of its field of action that Christian thought acquired the alliance of all these concepts and with it an entirely unexpected new wide field of activity.[88]

The question to be asked in regard to this movement of thought on the way to an affirmation of the "world come of age" and the elimination of the polemic against the world is whether or not these new, emerging features of Bonhoeffer's later thought derive in a significant way from Christological insight or development, and thus again whether the Christological theme is as formative as so many have argued.

To be sure, expressions of Christocentrism are very much in evidence in Bonhoeffer's *Ethics,* reflecting the continuation and even the accentuation of a "revelational positivism"—for example, the statement that "the world has no reality of its own, independently of the revelation of God in Christ."[89] But what, Christologically speaking, has triggered the sudden dropping of the Sermon on the Mount as a focus of Bonhoeffer's theological and personal reflection? or what has led to the abandonment of his position of pacifism?[90] There are unresolved tensions in the writings that make up the *Ethics,* tensions that suggest not only thought in flux, but, much more, a continuation of the personal quest, the quest that called forth later the anguished but resolute prison poem, "Who Am I?"

Between *The Cost of Discipleship* and *Ethics,* Christological movement is apparent. In place of the 1937 regal Christology calling for obedience, one encounters now the Christology of deputyship demanding "responsibility." Bonhoeffer writes:

> Jesus . . . lived in deputyship for us as the incarnate Son of God, and that is why through Him all human life is in essence a life of deputyship. Jesus was not the individual, desiring to achieve a perfection of his own, but He lived only as the one who has taken up into Himself and who bears within Himself the selves of all men. All His living, His action and His dying was deputyship. In Him there is fulfilled what the living, the action and the suffering of men ought to be. In this real deputyship which constitutes His human existence He is the responsible person par excellence. Because He is life all life is determined by Him to be deputyship.[91]

Responsibility is, for Bonhoeffer, action on behalf of others. It "lies only in the complete surrender of one's own life to the other man."[92] It means living on behalf of others as a "father acts for the children, working for them, caring for them, interceding, fighting and suffering for them."[93] This responsibility is not bound by the law:

> For the sake of God and of men Jesus became a breaker of the law. He broke the law of the Sabbath in order to keep it holy in love for God and for men. . . . Thus it is Jesus Christ who sets conscience free for the service of God and our neighbour; He sets conscience free, even and especially when man enters into the fellowship of human guilt. . . . The conscience which has been set free is not timid like the conscience which is bound by the law, but it stands wide open for our neighbour and for his concrete distress. And so conscience joins with the responsibility which has its foundation in Christ in bearing guilt for the sake of our neighbour.[94]

This Christology of deputyship represents a shift away from the
regal Christology of *The Cost of Discipleship*, but there is a continuation of both the cosmocratic motif and the imitation of Christ
found in the earlier work. The former motif is developed especially
in relation to the concept of the "divine mandates" in which Bonhoeffer sought to establish a ground in Christ for the social forms
of marriage and the family, culture, and government,[95] a Christocentric interpretation of the Lutheran "orders of preservation."[96]
In *The Cost of Discipleship*, Bonhoeffer asserted that Christ as
Mediator intervened between the believer, the disciple, and all
forms of immediacy in relation to persons *or things;*[97] now, in
Ethics, this mediatorial role is expressed in terms of Christ's
grounding of all of life[98] and bears meaning for the realm of social
ethics (the mandates) in contrast to the earlier stress upon the
individualistic ethics of discipleship.

If in *The Cost of Discipleship* the demands of *sola gratia* (by
grace alone) dictated a qualification of the imitation of Christ by
means of the concept of "conformation," the idea that at the same
time one emulates Christ one is *conformed* to Christ (by God, the
Holy Spirit), in the *Ethics* this theme is very much enlarged and
expanded. Conformation becomes a major theme of a portion of
the *Ethics*[99]—though there is a continuation also of the idea of
identification with the sufferings of Christ. The chief point of difference from the earlier discussion in *The Cost of Discipleship* is that
now suffering is interpreted no longer as a result of the world's
enmity but as a result of participation in the world's guilt.[100] In fact,
Christ's work bears this same shift in emphasis—from "obedience"
to the will of God as defined by the Sermon on the Mount, with
its concomitant suffering of the world's enmity, to "responsibility"
and involvement in the world's torment and guilt. Of this discussion in the *Ethics* one has to ask if we are not in fact dealing with
a Christology of "adulthood" so to speak.[101]

These examples of Christological thought from the *Ethics* do
not exhaust the Christological variety to be found there. Another
important and very large section of *Ethics* discusses the question
of eschatology in terms of the "ultimate" and the "penultimate,"

a discussion that is also a movement away from the thought of *The Cost of Discipleship* in its affirmation of the world. But Bonhoeffer's Christological discussion in this context differs again in tone and spirit from the other patterns we have discussed and reasserts some of the classical themes of redemption and justification.[102] All these patterns, rather than suggesting a Christological development, reflect much more a note of uncertainty. Christological content often seems to be determined by the particular new thought that Bonhoeffer was intent on exploring.

This same sort of phenomenon is to be noted when one turns from the *Ethics* to the *Letters and Papers from Prison* and the last phase of Bonhoeffer's thought. The "new idea" that has stimulated Bonhoeffer's creative energies in the most provocative sections of the prison letters is Dilthey's autonomous world, the "world come of age." In *The Cost of Discipleship* one was called to struggle against the world. In the *Ethics* one was called to order and structure the world. In the *Letters and Papers from Prison* the world has itself become a new point of departure. Everything has to be rethought, as it were, in the light of this new reality. One needs a "non-religious interpretation of biblical concepts." "Religion" has been superseded, but Christology remains. The Christology that remains, however, is an enigmatic one.

There are two critical Christological statements to be found in the prison letters, one in the letter of July 16, 1944, and the other in "Outline for a Book."[103] The most puzzling of the two is the former, which is set in the context of Bonhoeffer's argument against a false apologetic that seeks to exploit man's need and calls upon the *deus ex machina.* In this passage, which has already been touched upon, Bonhoeffer writes:

> The God who lets us live in the world without the working hypothesis of God is the God before whom we stand continually. Before God and with God we live without God. God lets himself be pushed out of the world on to the cross. He is weak and powerless in the world, and that is precisely the way, the only way, in which he is with us and helps us. Matt. 8.17 makes it quite clear that Christ helps us, not by virtue of his omnipotence, but by virtue of his weakness and suffering. . . . The

> Bible directs man to God's powerlessness and suffering; only the suffering God can help.[104]

The passage from Matt., ch. 8, that is referred to here reads: "This was to fulfil what was spoken by the prophet Isaiah, 'He took our infirmities and bore our diseases.' " The words would seem to represent a statement of Christ's vicarious atonement; but Bonhoeffer argues concerning "the world come of age" that it is an age in which questions about death and guilt may well lose their urgency,[105] and therefore it is difficult to conceive how God's helping "man come of age" could be construed other than in terms of moral example. At another point Bonhoeffer declares: "The Christian, unlike the devotees of the redemption myths, has no last line of escape available from earthly tasks and difficulties into the eternal, but, like Christ himself ('My God, why hast thou forsaken me?') he must drink the earthly cup to the dregs, and only in his doing so is the crucified and risen Lord with him, and he crucified and risen with Christ."[106]

When one turns to consider the second major Christological passage in "Outline for a Book," little is said there that would alter the dominant impression of an imitation of Christ.[107] That Bonhoeffer speaks of a "participation in the being of Jesus" does not significantly modify the exemplary character of that life, especially when Bonhoeffer equates Jesus' "being there for others" with the experience of transcendence. It is not surprising that Phillips should view the imitation of Christ as a chief feature of Bonhoeffer's later thought[108] and that Barth should describe Bonhoeffer's "sharing in the suffering of God" as "clearly a variation of the idea of *imitatio.*"[109]

Hanfried Müller makes much of a break in thought between *Ethics* and *Letters and Papers from Prison* and goes on to represent this break as the substitution of a theology of the cross for an earlier theology of exaltation. Also, Regin Prenter, a Danish theologian, impressively traces parallels between the thought of the young Luther and Bonhoeffer, reading the latter in the light of the former. Prenter offers an interpretation of Bonhoeffer that builds on the complementary relationship (in Luther) between a theology of the word and a theology of the cross.[110] But both Müller and Prenter leave out of account an explication of the occasion of Christ's suffering which, at least in the prison letters, is only very tenuously related to the question of sin.[111] When this point is clearly perceived, the so-called "parallels" between the young Luther and Bonhoeffer are much less compelling.

With regard to Feil's contribution to the Christological discussion, i.e., the description of Bonhoeffer's Christological movement from an early concentration on the meaning of Christ "for us" (the writings up through *The Cost of Discipleship* and *Life Together*) to an enlarged vision of the Christ "for others"—this interpretation suffers from a too-unquestioning acceptance of Bethge's "conversion" hypothesis and thus overemphasizes Bonhoeffer's supposedly conclusive subordination of the *actus reflexus* (reflection) to the *actus directus* (faith). Thus Feil fails to show the same acute, critical analysis of Bonhoeffer's post 1931–1932 writings that he displays toward the earliest (e.g., *The Communion of Saints*). He leaves the impression that Bonhoeffer's thought leads on (after 1931–1932) to ever more complete or substantial positions.[112] But one can as well argue that actually the real issue continues to be faith, with more than a modicum of Christological uncertainty.

THE REALITY THEME

Of the three themes that are most frequently cited as lending unity and coherence to Bonhoeffer's thought, the most tenuous of all is the "reality" (or "concretion") theme. While it is clear that the concern for reality, or concretion, manifests itself throughout the course of Bonhoeffer's theological work, this particular theme is probably more a symptom of uncertainty and an occasion for unpredictable shifts than it is a formative factor lending structural unity. In other words, it reflects more the character of Bonhoeffer's personal quest than a process of established and maturing thought. In Bonhoeffer's earlier work the concern for "concretion" is in large measure furthered by the logic of his polemic against idealism, but thereafter with the accent on the "who" of Christ in the Christology lectures, and on discipleship in *The Cost of Discipleship* (a means toward the reality of Christ), the particulars of Bonhoeffer's quest seem to supply the varying content of what he defines as "concrete" or "real." Rather than expressing assured certainty, such statements in the *Ethics* as "All concepts of reality which do not take account of [Jesus Christ] are abstractions"[113] or "It is from the real man, whose name is Jesus Christ, that all factual reality derives its ultimate foundation"[114] bear a certain wistful and at the same time heroic character. They are hardly to be interpreted as established points of departure. While it can be argued that the later question, "Who is Jesus Christ for us today?" is again only an insistence upon the concreteness of Christ,[115] this question in the *Letters and Papers from Prison* is raised in the context of Bonhoeffer's new convictions concerning the "world come of age" and stands in contrast to major assertions in the *Ethics* in which "reality" is to be seen only in Christ. It is in fact this sort of shift which leads Mayer to speak of the collapse of Bonhoeffer's "ontological system" between the *Ethics* and the prison letters.

While one can credit a certain viability to the interpretative approach to Bonhoeffer that allows an interplay of "faith" and "worldliness," or "Christ and world"—in contrast to the ontological interpretations of Ott, Mayer, and Dumas—to pursue such a pattern of interpretation demands great care in the definition of the polar opposite of faith and in how one goes about defining that polar reality. One simply cannot presuppose agreement on what constitutes reality, or "worldliness," either within the intellectual community, the day-to-day working community, or the community of faith. Paul Lehmann, himself an advocate of the "faith-worldliness" interpretation, comments trenchantly: "Freud and his disciples and correctors are but the latest documenters of the fact that the 'reality principle' has always had hard going in a world in which illusions are hard to break and fulfilling loyalties hard to come by."[116] And Dumas, despite his rather contradictory assertion of a structural ontology as the basis of Bonhoeffer's thought, makes the observation that Bonhoeffer's insistence upon a concretion of place (a kind of "reality principle") moves from the affirmation of state church (and "Christendom") to Confessing Church to the church of "non-religious interpretation" and "secret discipline."[117] Certainly the "reality principle" allows a description of impulsiveness and unexpected turnings in Bonhoeffer's thought as much as it does an assertion of coherence and unity.

From this assessment of the supposed unifying themes of Bonhoeffer's theology the conclusion is unavoidable that more has been claimed for Bonhoeffer's theology than critical analysis has been able to establish. In the early 1950's Barth noted the tendency of Bonhoeffer to pick up on a theme, develop it at times in an impressive manner, but then move on to some other concern.[118] There are certainly grounds for this complaint: preoccupation with the Sermon on the Mount, then after 1939 virtual abandonment of it, Bonhoeffer's own negative attitude toward his early *Act and Being,* his ecclesiocentrism modified by "free church" impulses, his confessionalism yielding to an "unconscious Christianity," his seeming abandonment of the concept of the mandates in the prison letters, the embrace and then rejection of pacificism, shifting assessments of the nature and cause of suffering, his temporary fascination with institutional forms and liturgy, and his experiments with a corporate discipline. We have suggested that the movement of Bonhoeffer's thought is best understood as the interplay of the logic of a transcendent revelation (later rejected as "revelational positivism")[119] and a personal quest for faith and spiritual certainty. The "logic" structured and channeled the quest for a while, but then, increasingly, the quest, conditioned naturally by unique personal circumstances and the historical situation, broke free to pursue its own course. Set against this possible reading of the Bonhoeffer legacy, the lines of continuity that are traceable in Bonhoeffer's thought are not as compelling as the earnest uncertainties of the quest. This becomes an even more plausible explanation of Bonhoeffer's odyssey when one understands that the forms of conceptualization are not easily shaken in the intellectual life and frequently are made the bearers of important shifts in thinking that are not immediately apparent.

The question that remains to be asked is whether this "quest" interpretation of Bonhoeffer's life and thought is an exaggeration of the subjective dimension and a kind of argument *ad hominem* that disallows a fair reading of the materials, or whether in fact it permits an even more compelling picture of the whole. But before a judgment is made on this matter, a somewhat neglected part of the whole must be spelled out in order that new perspective may perhaps be gained.

❦ 5 ❦

Complication
of the Quest:
The Aristocratic,
Vitalistic Motif

In a review of the 1970 English edition of Bethge's biography, John Godsey, the first to offer a full-length study of Bonhoeffer's thought, raises a troublesome and nagging question. He writes: "My real question is this: Did he (Bonhoeffer) do what he did because of his Christian convictions or because of the inbred and inculcated qualities derived from his unusual family? In the final analysis, what distinguishes him from his brother Klaus ar.d his two brothers-in-law, all of whom also entered into the resistance and paid with their lives?"[1]

This question is not just some quirk of curiosity on Godsey's part. It is a question that arises out of the very substance of the Bonhoeffer materials. It is a haunting question that even the closest of Bonhoeffer's friends are prone, it seems, to ask—perhaps not directly, in the terms of Godsey, but at least implicitly. For example, Paul Lehmann comments on Bonhoeffer's "aristocracy of spirit":

> His aristocracy was unmistakable yet not obtrusive, chiefly, I think, owing to his boundless curiosity about every new environment in which he found himself and to his irresistible and unfailing sense of humour. Thus he could suggest without offence that we should not play tennis

together since he commanded a certain expertness at the game which
I could not claim.[2]

Also, Lehmann speaks of Bonhoeffer's fascination with the Spanish
bullfight: "As I recall among our own disputes and debates . . . in
the seminary as fellow students, the thing I never could really get
through my mind was that this Lutheran Christian was absolutely
ecstatic about the bullfights. He thought that the bullfights in Spain
were one of the most exciting aspects of what he learned there."[3]

As further illustration of Bonhoeffer's attraction to a vitalistic
expression of life,[4] Johannes Goebel, a seminarian at Finkenwalde,
remarks upon Bonhoeffer's subordination of his musical skills to
his theological commitment. Goebel speaks of once asking the
talented Bonhoeffer "whether he had ever tried, or was trying, to
compose anything. In a distinctly reserved tone he said he had
stopped doing so since he had become a theologian, or something
to the effect."[5] Goebel then comments:

> That it was a "casting out" is quite clear to me from a picture which
> rises in my memory. While he was sitting at the piano something which
> I had not known in him and have never seen again, an expression of
> natural force, of something primeval, came over him, a Dietrich differ-
> ent from the one known to us. It was not just his natural freshness, his
> energy, his will power. . . . [His] playing was hard, he hammered away,
> too loud. I do not, unfortunately, remember the musical style of his
> improvisation; probably because it fascinated me more to witness the
> native human quality breaking through his personality, than to pay
> attention to his music. And suddenly he stopped as abruptly as he had
> begun.[6]

Also, Bonhoeffer's father once described to his son his reservations about the latter's decision to take up the study of theology.
In a 1934 letter the father wrote: "At the time when you decided
to devote yourself to theology I sometimes thought to myself that
a quiet, uneventful, minister's life . . . would really almost be a pity
for you."[7]

All the testimonies to Bonhoeffer's vitalistic propensities, his
inner strength, his impressive presence, would be unimportant if

they did not have a bearing upon the interpretation of his thought, or find some echo in his theological formulation. In fact, they do. Other interpreters have taken note of Bonhoeffer's "aristocratic nature" and have used this assessment of Bonhoeffer in argument and counterargument while projecting very varied interpretations of Bonhoeffer's thought.[8]

Heinrich Ott, for example, cites Bonhoeffer's aristocratic outlook as a fundamental motive behind his search for a "non-religious interpretation of biblical concepts" and on this basis scorns Hanfried Müller's effort to transpose Bonhoeffer's later "non-religious" interest into a Marxist frame of reference. Far from finding in Bonhoeffer's later writings a firm grasp of new social and historical realities, as Müller would have it, Ott discerns only a "wavering" and "indefinite" picture of "the course of the Western world." Ott declares:

> It was a field in which [Bonhoeffer] was experimenting. But by contrast, in his statement of his postulate of a non-religious interpretation, he seems to be completely sure of his facts. Surely it follows clearly enough from this that this postulate has been nourished at other springs, that behind it are other motives, another and much stronger foundation, than merely a certain theoretical judgment on the course of history.[9]

Ott grounds Bonhoeffer's later thoughts about the "non-religious interpretation of biblical concepts" on Bonhoeffer's aristocratic, uncompromising confrontation with the reality of his time (the "world come of age").[10] He concludes: "In [the] harmony of aristocratic manliness, thisworldliness and human realism we once again detect, perhaps at its purest in the latest period of his life, the keynote of Bonhoeffer's theological existence."[11]

On a different point, but again in reaction to Müller's interpretation, John Phillips also cites Bonhoeffer's aristocratic demeanor and outlook. Over against Müller, who insists on the close relationship of Bonhoeffer's theological statements to the political and social situation, Phillips accents "the 'aristocratic' Bonhoeffer, [whose] *freedom* from time and place and circumstance characterized him beyond all else and astonishes all who read the prison letters."[12] Phillips goes on to argue that this fact of Bonhoeffer's independence of time and place ought to govern the methodology of Bonhoeffer interpretation.[13]

Rainer Mayer adds still another dimension to the observations about Bonhoeffer's "aristocratic" inclination by suggesting that his later turn away from the Confessing Church was in large degree precipitated by his contacts with the men of the German resistance movement. Mayer writes:

> What Bonhoeffer misses in the Confessing Church, he finds very much present, even though in quite a different form, in the circle of the Resistance movement centered around Dohnanyi and Oster. Here are men who stand up for truth and right without compromise, though in danger of their lives. Here there are genuine worldliness in responsible act, a knowledge of reality free of ideology, representation and engagement on behalf of others. They are people who hold the necessary act in higher esteem than the unsullied conscience. Moreover, one is certain that if one asked about their motives, none of them would name Christian faith. Bonhoeffer learned from these responsible, mature men that there are inner-worldly constraints against evil and annihilation and that one is not dependent only upon the church for finding the concrete commandment for the actual historical situation. . . .[14]

To be sure, Mayer balances this observation about Bonhoeffer's experiential involvement and the direction it implies for Bonhoeffer's later conceptual development ("world come of age," "non-religious interpretation," "unconscious Christianity," etc.) with the assertion of an equally important role for Bonhoeffer's ontological concerns,[15] but the suggestion of Bonhoeffer's crucial exposure to aristocratic, "mature" humanity is significant. Hans Christoph von Hase, whom Mayer cites at this point, speaks of Bonhoeffer's encounter in the Resistance with a type of man who was not unknown to Bonhoeffer earlier and who forced Bonhoeffer to reconsider his thought about the church.[16]

These lines of argument and interpretation suggest a not insignificant role for Bonhoeffer's aristocratic background and associations. But up to now interpreters who have taken note of this aspect of Bonhoeffer's character and outlook have generally viewed it in a benign fashion. They have used it as a corrective to forced ideological analysis (such as that of Müller) and as a source of helpful insight into aspects of Bonhoeffer's later thought.[17] The possibility exists, however, that this aristocratic tendency in Bonhoeffer is much more than a benign or secondary matter, that its presence throughout his life was an occasion of restlessness and uncertainty, and that it greatly influenced the pattern of his quest for faith. In short, the possibility exists that major light can be shed upon the dynamics of Bonhoeffer's thought by paying stricter heed to the fundamental character of the anthropological question and Bonhoeffer's own quest for spiritual identity. A review of the strength/weakness motif in Bonhoeffer's thought is an important step in this direction.

THE STRENGTH/WEAKNESS THEME

In one of Bonhoeffer's last letters to Bethge, the letter of August 21, 1944, there is a moving statement of Bonhoeffer's perseverance in faith—which we have already quoted in part.[18] He remarks:

All that we may rightly expect from God, and ask him for, is to be found in Jesus Christ. The God of Jesus Christ has nothing to do with what God, as we imagine him, could do and ought to do. If we are to learn what God promises, and what he fulfills, we must persevere in quiet meditation on the life, sayings, deeds, sufferings, and death of Jesus. It is certain that we may always live close to God and in the light of his presence, and that such living is an entirely new life for us; that nothing is then impossible for us, because all things are possible with God; that no earthly power can touch us without his will, and that danger and distress can only drive us closer to him.[19]

The statement is noteworthy chiefly for its rather traditional content. The piety expressed here is far from revolutionary; and it is hard to see, in the light of a world come of age, how anything has changed. Then, however, as if to balance the traditional tone, Bonhoeffer ends the letter with an additional note:

> Another point: we are often told in the New Testament to "be strong" (I Cor. 16.13, Eph. 6.10; II Tim. 2.1; I John 2.14). Isn't people's weakness (stupidity, lack of independence, forgetfulness, cowardice, vanity, corruptibility, temptability, etc.) a greater danger than evil? Christ not only makes people "good," he makes them strong, too. The sins of weakness are the really human sins, whereas the wilful sins are diabolical (and no doubt "strong," too!). I must think about this again.[20]

The strength/weakness motif is very much in evidence through the course of Bonhoeffer's prison writings. It is no minor theme but seems always present, demanding expression in one form or another, and is intimately related to an aristocratic, heroic outlook. In the letter of August 10, 1944, Bonhoeffer writes: "It is weakness rather than wickedness that perverts a man and drags him down. . . ."[21] Among the "miscellaneous thoughts" jotted down in prison is the statement: "It is the nature, and the advantage, of strong people that they can bring out the crucial questions and form a clear opinion about them. The weak always have to decide between alternatives that are not their own."[22] In "Stations on the Road to Freedom," Bonhoeffer writes: "Daring to do what is right, not what fancy may tell you, valiantly grasping occasions, not cravenly doubting—freedom comes only through deeds, not through thoughts taking wing. Faint not nor fear, but go out to the storm and the action, trusting in God whose commandment you faithfully follow. . . ."[23] And at another point Bonhoeffer's attack upon "inwardness" focuses upon "a revolt of inferiority." The vehemence of Bonhoeffer's words is startling. He writes:

> The displacement of God from the world, and from the public part of life, led to the attempt to keep his place secure at least in the sphere of the "personal," the "inner," and the "private." And as every man still has a private sphere somewhere, that is where he was thought to be the most vulnerable. The secrets known to a man's valet—that is,

to put it crudely, the range of his intimate life—have become the hunting-ground of modern pastoral workers. In that way they resemble . . . the dirtiest gutter journalists. . . . From the sociological point of view this is a revolution from below, a revolt of inferiority. Just as the vulgar mind isn't satisfied till it has seen some highly placed personage "in his bath," or in other embarrassing situations, so it is here. There is a kind of evil satisfaction in knowing that everyone has his failings and weak spots.[24]

And again, in the letter of June 8, 1944, Bonhoeffer follows up a criticism of Christian apologetics with an attack on "existentialist philosophy and the psychotherapists who demonstrate to secure, contented, and happy mankind that it is really unhappy and desperate and simply unwilling to admit that it is in a predicament about which it knows nothing, and from which only they can rescue it. Wherever there is health, strength, security, simplicity, they scent luscious fruit to gnaw at or lay their pernicious eggs in."[25] And whom does this "secularized methodism" touch? Bonhoeffer answers: "A small number of intellectuals, of degenerates, of people who regard themselves as the most important thing in the world, and who therefore like to busy themselves with themselves."[26] Bonhoeffer declares that "the importunity" of the existentialists and psychotherapists is "far too unaristocratic for the Word of God to ally itself with them."[27]

The presence of the strength/weakness theme and its corollary, the "aristocratic"/"unaristocratic" motif, is especially noteworthy in the letters from April 30, 1944, onward. It plays a basic role in the definition of the "world come of age," in Bonhoeffer's attack upon "inwardness" and "religion," in his probings of an "unconscious Christianity," in his rejection of the past history of Christian apologetics, his representation of the *deus ex machina,* and his reappraisal of the Old Testament.[28] It is also of fundamental significance in Bonhoeffer's continued groping for an understanding of faith. In the letter of July 18, 1944, Bonhoeffer writes: "To be a Christian does not mean to be religious in a particular way, to make something of oneself (a sinner, a penitent, or a saint) on the basis of some method or other, but to be a man—not a type of man, but the man that Christ creates in us. It is not the religious act that makes the Christian, but participation in the sufferings of God in the secular life. That is *metanoia* ["repentance"]: not in the first place thinking about one's own needs, problems, sins, and fears, but allowing oneself to be caught up into the way of Jesus Christ; into the messianic event, thus fulfilling Is. 53."[29] Referring then to certain figures in the New Testament, Bonhoeffer declares: "The eunuch (Acts 8) and Cornelius (Acts 10) are not standing at the edge of an abyss. Nathaniel is 'an Israelite indeed, in whom there is no guile' (John 1.47). . . . The only thing that is common to all these is their sharing in the suffering of God in Christ. That is their 'faith.' "[30] Then, three days later and one day after the failure of the plot to assassinate Hitler, Bonhoeffer writes: "By this-worldliness I mean living unreservedly in life's duties, problems, successes and failures, experiences and perplexities. In so doing we throw ourselves completely into the arms of God, taking seriously, not our own sufferings, but those of God in the world—watching with Christ in Gethsemane. That, I think, is faith, that is *metanoia;* and that is how one becomes a man and a Christian (cf. Jer. 45!)."[31] Shortly thereafter, Bonhoeffer turns again to the subject of faith and says: "Not only action, but also suffering is a way to freedom. In suffering, the deliverance consists in our being allowed to put the matter out of our own hands into God's hands. In this sense, death is the crowning of human freedom. Whether the human deed is a matter of faith or not depends on whether we understand our suffering as an extension of our action and a completion of freedom. I think that is very important and very comforting."[32]

There can be no question that "faith" here catches up the action motif, so basic to a vital, heroic spirit. It has, however, been leavened by a deep personal experience of suffering; and thus, by contrast with descriptions of faith in *Ethics,*[33] there is added a certain longing for comfort in the midst of the call to manhood. One cannot, I think, here exercise the logic of systematics and explicate definitively the ambiguous meaning of some of Bonhoeffer's formulations—especially the enigmatic statement that, in the midst of a "world come of age," "Christ helps us, not by virtue of his omnipotence, but by virtue of his weakness and suffering."[34] These are best understood as expressions of a troubled quest; they suggest a uniquely personal dimension of faith, and to fail to recognize this is to do injustice to what Bonhoeffer has left us.

Nevertheless, one must be clear about the importance of the strength/weakness theme in Bonhoeffer's thought. This theme comes to its most potent expression in the thought of the later prison letters, but one must note its significant presence *throughout* Bonhoeffer's writings.

In the earlier letters from prison, those before April 30, 1944, the theme is associated with many of Bonhoeffer's observations about prison life and his own introspective reflections.[35] It figures in his discussion of *hilaritas* as the mark of great men (e.g., Luther, Lessing, Rubens, Hugo Wolf, Karl Barth): *hilaritas,* Bonhoeffer asserts, is "confidence in [one's] own work, boldness and defiance of the world and of popular opinion, a steadfast certainty. . . ."[36] It is present in his views on culture (*Bildung*): "The only thing I am really clear about in the whole problem is that a 'culture' that breaks down in the face of danger is no culture. Culture must be able to face danger and death . . . even if it cannot 'conquer' them."[37] The matter of culture, education, family background and the strength they afford one is the subject of a dramatic piece that Bonhoeffer wrote in 1943. The theme of this play was a favorite of Bonhoeffer's: the need to have "ground under one's feet."[38] A variation of this same strength/weakness theme is present also in a paper entitled "After Ten Years," which Bonhoeffer circulated among his friends shortly before his arrest. The paper calls for "responsible action in a bold venture of faith"[39] and a recovery of "the lost sense of quality."[40]

In *Ethics,* Bonhoeffer's aristocratic outlook and his attraction for the strength/weakness theme is only slightly less manifest than in the *Letters and Papers from Prison.* One is confronted with the aristocratic point of view in Bonhoeffer's insistence

upon the recognition of "superiority" and "inferiority" within
the human community. He points to a

> disparity which is so extremely offensive to modern sensibilities but
> which is inherent and essential in the ethical, namely, the disparity
> between the superior and the inferior. Without this objective subordi-
> nation of the lower to the higher, and without that courage to accept
> superiority which modern man has so completely lost, ethical discourse
> is dissipated in generalities, it lacks an object and its essential character
> is destroyed. The ethical, therefore, is not a principle which levels out,
> invalidates and disrupts the whole order of human precedence and
> subordination, but already in itself it implies a definite structure of
> human society; it implies certain definite sociological relations which
> involve authority.[41]

Bonhoeffer says that the disparity within human society between
"superior" and "inferior" is a *sine qua non* of "serious" ethical
discourse. In point of fact, this disparity underlies Bonhoeffer's
understanding of responsibility and the action of certain individu-
als "on behalf of," or "for," others.[42] In another discussion in the
Ethics, "History and Good," Bonhoeffer states: "And so it seems
that everything that we have said about responsibility can in the
end apply only to a very small group of men, and even to those only
in a few moments of their lives; and consequently it seems as
though for the great majority of men one must speak not of responsibility but of obedience and duty. This implies one ethic for the
great and the strong, for the rulers, and another for the small and
the weak, the subordinates; on the one hand responsibility and on
the other obedience, on the one hand freedom and on the other
subservience."[43] However, not satisfied with this restriction of responsibility, *but at the same time not denying the basic order of
superiority/inferiority,* Bonhoeffer goes on to argue for a wider
application of responsibility than that suggested by the external
orders of society and the formal exercise of power. He writes:
"Even when free responsibility is more or less excluded from a
man's vocational and public life, he nevertheless always stands in
a responsible relation to other men; these relations extend from his

family to his workmates. The fulfilment of genuine responsibility at this point affords the only sound possibility of extending the sphere of responsibility once more into vocational and public life. Where man meets man—and this includes the encounters of professional life—there arises genuine responsibility, and these responsible relationships cannot be supplanted by any general regulation or routine."[44]

Set as some of these arguments are in the context of Bonhoeffer's teaching on "the mandates," it is important to note that in *Ethics* the grounding of all this (the call to responsibility and obedience) lies in the personal commandment of God. Bonhoeffer asserts that the divine mandates (marriage, culture, government, church) are "dependent solely on the *one* commandment of God as it is revealed in Jesus Christ. They are introduced into the world from above as orders or 'institutions' of the reality of Christ. . . . This means that they are not in any sense products of history; they are not earthly powers, but divine commissions."[45] "This means," Bonhoeffer continues, "that the commandment of God wishes to find man always in an earthly relation of authority, in a clearly defined order of superiority and inferiority."[46] Bonhoeffer goes on to clarify his own understanding and use of the terms "superiority" and "inferiority," insisting that "the stronger can certainly not without further ado claim for himself the authority of the divine mandate *vis-à-vis* the weaker."[47] Rather, "it is characteristic of the divine mandate that it corrects and regulates the earthly relations of superior and inferior power in its own way."[48] "The master, too, has a Master, and this fact alone establishes his right to be master and authorizes and legitimates his relation to the servant."[49] In Bonhoeffer's whole discussion of the mandates the aristocratic motif is wedded to a kind of nonhistorical, hierarchical world view reminiscent of the medieval, in which "the genuine order of superior and inferior draws its life from belief in the commission from 'above,' belief in the 'Lord of lords.' This belief alone can exorcize the demonic forces which emerge from below. The collapse of this belief means the total collapse and destruction of the whole structure and order which is established in the world from above."[50]

If there is present in the *Ethics* a hierarchical ordering of life, there is also an effort made to define Christian existence in a dialectical ("yes/no") manner. In this latter undertaking—one not wholly consistent with the hierarchical viewpoint—the strength/ weakness theme is transposed into a vitalistic one and becomes the dialectical opposite of asceticism, even though the latter also entails a certain heroic discipline. Bonhoeffer sees both alternatives, the "yes" and the "no" of life, united in Christ. The former is "the 'yes' to what is created, to becoming and to growth, to the flower and the fruit, to health, happiness, ability, achievement, worth, success, greatness and honour; in short, it is the 'yes' to the development of the power of life."[51] But because life is marred by a certain "defection from its origin" (i.e., sin), there must also be a "no," and this "means dying, suffering, poverty, renunciation, resignation, humility, degradation, self-denial."[52] However, since there is a unity of these in Christ the two opposites cannot be viewed simply as alternative spheres, "an unrestrained expansion of vitality" existing "side by side with a wholly separate ascetic and spiritual attitude, . . . [a] 'creaturely' conduct side by side with 'Christian' conduct."[53] The strong tendency in Bonhoeffer to want to hold these two patterns together is elsewhere evident: "Being loved by God does not by any means deprive man of his mighty thoughts and his spirited deeds";[54] and again: "In . . . confinement within the limits of duty there can never come the bold stroke of the deed which is done on one's own free responsibility, the only kind of deed which can strike at the heart of evil and overcome it."[55] One should also point out that in offering exposition of the important terms "ultimate" and "penultimate," Bonhoeffer adopts an anthropocentric approach that similarly envisions a reconciliation of justification by grace (ultimate) with good works (penultimate).[56]

When one moves from the *Ethics* to *Life Together* and *The Cost of Discipleship,* works preceding Bonhoeffer's involvement in the underground conspiracy against Hitler, one is especially impressed by Bonhoeffer's earlier quest for faith. Apparent also is the logic of revelation that helped to channel and direct that earlier quest. For example, in *Life Together* Bonhoeffer declares—and one cannot but surmise that the statement is autobiographical: "It is not the experience of Christian brotherhood, but solid and certain faith in brotherhood that holds us together. That God has acted and wants to act upon us all, this we see in faith as God's greatest gift, this makes us glad and happy, but it also makes us ready to forego all such experiences when God at times does not grant them. We are bound together by faith, not by experience."[57] Other similar statements indicate the personal character of Bonhoeffer's quest.[58] And something of this quest is also to be noted in the emphasis he placed on confession during this period of his life.[59] Bonhoeffer writes: "In confession the break-through to community takes place. . . . In confession occurs the break-through to the Cross. . . . In confession the break-through to new life occurs. . . . Confession is discipleship. . . . In confession a man breaks through to certainty. . . ."[60]

But amid this earlier search for faith—or spiritual certainty—Bonhoeffer also is caught up with the question of strength and weakness, an accent no doubt explicable, in part at least, by the realities of the church struggle. But still, its prevalence and the weight given to it are striking. Bonhoeffer states at one point: "Every Christian community must realize that not only do the weak need the strong, but also that the strong cannot exist without the weak. The elimination of the weak is the death of fellowship."[61] And again: "Has the fellowship served to make the individual free, strong, and mature, or has it made him weak and dependent? Has it taken him by the hand for a while in order that he may learn again to walk by himself, or has it made him uneasy and unsure? This is one of the most searching and critical questions that can be put to any Christian fellowship."[62]

Bonhoeffer further notes that in human community, in contrast to spiritual community, there generally occurs a "forcing of another person into one's sphere of power and influence. Here is where the humanly strong person is in his element, securing for himself the admiration, the love, or the fear of the weak."[63] Bonhoeffer warns that this can occur within the Christian community. "It appears in all the forms of conversion wherever the superior power of one person is consciously or unconsciously misused to influence profoundly and draw into his spell another individual or a whole community. . . . The weak have been overcome by the strong, the resistance of the weak has broken down under the influence of another person. He has been overpowered, but not won over by the thing itself."[64] In these and other passages that could be cited[65] it can be seen that even in *Life Together* the matter of strength and weakness is a significant motif, and one is forced to surmise that its peculiar persistence in this study of Christian community reflects Bonhoeffer's special attraction to this definition of manhood.

An analysis of *The Cost of Discipleship* yields similar conclusions. Here, even though the terminology was especially influenced by Bonhoeffer's parallel Kierkegaard studies[66] and, by comparison with *Life Together,* gives less prominence to the "strength/weakness" motif, the thought itself bears a similar accent. However, instead of speaking of "strength" and "weakness," Bonhoeffer develops his argument in terms of the categories of "costly grace" and "cheap grace."

In the introduction to *The Cost of Discipleship,* Bonhoeffer remarks:

> But one question still troubles us. What can the call to discipleship mean today for the worker, the businessman, the squire and the soldier? Does it not lead to an intolerable dichotomy between our lives as workers in the world and our lives as Christians? If Christianity means following Christ, is it not a religion for a small minority, a spiritual elite? Does it not mean the repudiation of the great mass of society and a hearty contempt for the weak and the poor? Yet surely such an attitude is the exact opposite of the gracious mercy of Jesus Christ, who came to the publicans and sinners, the weak and the poor, the erring and the hopeless. Are those who belong to Jesus only a few, or are they many?"[67]

Bonhoeffer never explicitly answers this question—either in the continuation of the paragraph or in the book as a whole. He *does* assert that the gospel reaches men in differing roles and conditions, but as to the question of "few" or "many" the drift in Bonhoeffer's thought is clearly in the direction of the former.[68] Thus, in his interpretation of Luther's turn from the monastery to the world, Bonhoeffer insists that, in monasticism, the limitation of obedience to Christ's commandments to the few imposed "a fatal conception of the double standard," a maximum and a minimum obedience, which Luther rejected.[69] Luther, Bonhoeffer argues, came to see that "the following of Christ is not the achievement or merit of a select few, but the divine commandment to all Christians without distinction."[70] This apparently forthright rejection of spiritual elitism is, however, obscured when Bonhoeffer argues that actually monasticism was simply a reflection of the world's standards and that

> the renunciation [Luther] made when he became a monk was child's play compared with that which he had to make when he returned to the world. . . . Hitherto the Christian life had been the achievement of a few choice spirits under the exceptionally favourable conditions of monasticism; now it is a duty laid on every Christian living in the world. The commandment of Jesus must be accorded perfect obedience in one's daily vocation of life. The conflict between the life of the Christian and the life of the world was thus thrown into the sharpest possible relief. It was a hand-to-hand conflict between the Christian and the world.[71]

Bonhoeffer then continues: "It is a fatal misunderstanding of Luther's action to suppose that his rediscovery of the gospel of pure grace offered a general dispensation from obedience to the command of Jesus, or that it was the great discovery of the Reformation that God's forgiving grace automatically conferred upon the world both righteousness and holiness. On the contrary, for Luther the Christian's worldly calling is sanctified only in so far as that calling registers the final radical protest against the world."[72] And Bonhoeffer goes on to argue that Luther's understanding of grace was that of a "costly grace" because, "far from dispensing him from good works, it meant that he must take the call to discipleship more seriously than ever before. It was grace because it cost so much, and it cost so much because it was grace."[73] In this vein

Bonhoeffer declares: "The only man who has the right to say that he is justified by grace alone is the man who has left all to follow Christ."[74]

It is not at all surprising to find Bonhoeffer saying later in *The Cost of Discipleship* that not only does God uphold and preserve the world for the sake of the church (the few),[75] but even within the church there are "some" to whom Christ "vouchsafes the immeasurable grace and privilege of suffering 'for him,' as he did for them. No greater glory could he have granted to his own . . . than to suffer 'for Christ.' "[76] Bonhoeffer continues: "Whether we have any right to assume that this suffering has power to atone for sin (cf. I Pet. 4.1), we have no means of knowing. But we do at least know that the man who suffers in the power of the body of Christ suffers in a representative capacity 'for' the church, the Body of Christ, being privileged to endure himself what others are spared."[77] The ambiguity and uncertainty that surrounds Bonhoeffer's attitude toward the imitation of Christ[78] is paralleled here by the ambiguity that surrounds the matter of the "few" and the "many." The supposition that we have in *The Cost of Discipleship* a "dialectic" is an inadequate description of Bonhoeffer's exposition.[79] Much more compelling is a reading and an understanding that is sensitive to the ambiguity and uncertainty that attended Bonhoeffer's own spiritual quest.[80]

In the earlier works as well one can trace the strength/weakness motif and its aristocratic corollary. But here it is less patent than in any of the later writings. There are at least two reasons for this. First, Bonhoeffer's own thought was just beginning to gain direction and there are many crosscurrents of thought and influence at work in both *The Communion of Saints* and *Act and Being*. And, secondly, the direction that *does* emerge in these discussions is what we have termed the "logic of revelation" (the rejection of natural theology and rationalism in favor of the affirmation of God's freedom in revelation). Bonhoeffer in these earlier works was becoming increasingly articulate in the statement and application of this logic; and there was much in Barth's challenging theological statement that attracted and satisfied the energies resident in the latent strength/weakness motif. Nevertheless, the presence of the strength/weakness motif is to be noted even in these works, especially in *The Communion of Saints.*[81] And in *Act and Being,* the frequency of the autobiographical statement suggests that the quest was then in process of taking shape.[82]

When to the documented presence of the strength/weakness motif in Bonhoeffer's major written works one adds his early fascination with Nietzsche's thought, one is forced to deal seriously with complicating factors in Bonhoeffer's quest for faith. The attraction to Nietzsche occurred in Bonhoeffer's student days and is to be noted as a strong influence in his early writings on the question of ethics. In a 1929 lecture on this subject, Nietzsche's influence is especially manifest. Bonhoeffer declared:

> The Christian himself creates his standards of good and evil for himself. Only he can justify his own actions, just as only he can bear the responsibility. The Christian creates new tables, a new Decalogue, as Nietzsche said of the Superman. Nietzsche's Superman is not really, as he supposed, the opposite of the Christian; without knowing it, Nietzsche has here introduced many traits of the Christian made free, as Paul and Luther describe him. Time-honoured morals—even if they are given out to be the consensus of Christian opinion—can never for the Christian become the standard of his actions. He acts, because the will of God seems to bid him to, without a glance at the others, at what is usually called morals, and no one but himself and God can know whether he has acted well or badly. In ethical decision we are brought into the deepest solitude, the solitude in which a man stands before the living God.[83]

On the matter of Nietzsche's influence on Bonhoeffer, Bethge has remarked: "Bonhoeffer read very carefully all of Nietzsche. Nietzsche's tremendous plea for the earth and the loyalty to its creatures never left Bonhoeffer's mind. The giant Antäus, who was strong as long as he had his feet on the earth, is in a speech of Bonhoeffer's as early as 1928 and is present again in a draft of a play written in prison in 1944. When Bonhoeffer assumed that Barth's philosophical background was neo-Kantianism, then his own was certainly colored by the terminology of the philosophy of life."[84]

Certainly it must be said of the strength/weakness motif in Bonhoeffer's thought that it is a very personal, existential motif and that it probably represents, at points, an unconscious motif, suggesting simply Bonhoeffer's own strong attraction to a forceful, vital understanding of manhood.[85] This motif plays a role not only in Bonhoeffer's quest for spiritual certainty but also in the forms of his theological conceptualization. The suggestion has been made that it introduces inner tensions into Bonhoeffer's thought that help to explain some of the peculiar turns of his later thinking, turns that are not explicable, not to be anticipated, on theological grounds alone. For example, the great variety of ways in which Bonhoeffer defines "faith" and "grace" over the course of his life,[86] the "heroic" character of Bonhoeffer's spirituality in *The Cost of Discipleship,* his lifelong fascination with death and martyrdom,[87] the turn from a lonely pacifism to involvement in the plot on Hitler's life: these aspects of Bonhoeffer's life and thought are much more understandable when viewed against the background of Bonhoeffer's personal struggle and quest.

PERSONAL CRISIS

The significance of this whole analysis can perhaps be more sharply defined if we take up an important feature of Feil's argument, the assertion that Bonhoeffer's later "world come of age" theme "is grounded *not* biographically in Bonhoeffer's personal development, but historically in a profound change of the times."[88] Feil declares that "coming-of-age is . . . not primarily a category of individual maturation, but a category of epochal, social emancipation."[89] This contention of Feil—with or without the qualifier "primarily" in the second statement—is to be challenged head-on.

As a first point, one is reminded that in Feil's argument regarding Bonhoeffer's shift from a theologically reflective attitude to an involved commitment, major emphasis is placed on Bethge's hypothesis regarding some sort of conversion experience during the years 1931–1932 ("The Theologian Becomes a Christian").[90] In connection with this hypothesis Feil indicates his agreement with

Bethge's contention that Bonhoeffer's 1930–1931 visit to America played a crucial role in the deepened commitment, stemming perhaps from Bonhoeffer's encounter with Jean Lasserre.[91] With Bethge, Feil asserts that the 1930–1931 American visit was "a more decisive turning point for Bonhoeffer than the short trip to America in 1939, even if the latter, perhaps in its clarity and its effect upon his subsequent destiny, is more eye-catching."[92] As previously noted, Feil presses his argument about a shift from the *actus reflexus* to the *actus directus* by offering an excursus in which he maintains that the movement from "thought" to "deed" is paralleled by Bonhoeffer's move from a purely academic vocation to increasing involvement in the ecclesiastical and pastoral sphere.[93] All of this, in Feil's analysis, is related to the problem of hermeneutics, the question about how best to interpret the reality of a sovereign and "hidden" God (and the Biblical materials testifying to him) when the possibility of man's inherent knowledge of God is excluded.[94]

At issue in Feil's argument—an issue already delineated[95]—is the dubious contention that although "conversion" and "ecclesiastical involvement" underlie and parallel Bonhoeffer's early change of thought from *actus reflexus* to *actus directus,* no such concrete, personal experience or crisis, according to Feil, underlies Bonhoeffer's later adoption of Dilthey's "world come of age." Feil notes that this intellectual "event," as it were, is grounded simply in an objective recognition of "epochal and social emancipation." A second point at issue is the significance attaching to Bonhoeffer's second visit to America in 1939 and the suggestion put forth by Feil and Bethge that the later visit was in no way as important as the first.

Over against Feil and Bethge, it seems at least as plausible to argue that Bonhoeffer's decision to return to Germany from America in 1939 is, in fact, a crucial turning point. And it was—existentially and theologically speaking—of equal if not greater significance than the first visit. It was this second visit and the issue it presented of his own motives for leaving Germany—the question of "piety" or flight—which underlies Bonhoeffer's later turn of thought in the direction of the "world come of age" and all of its attendant corollaries. What had been, prior to this time, a largely latent motif, the strength/weakness theme, became thereafter increasingly explicit and formative, leading even to Bonhoeffer's espousal of the possibility of an "aristocratic Christianity."[96]

An important dimension of this alternative interpretation is a review of Bonhoeffer's earlier departure from Germany, not the first trip to America, but the journey to London in October 1933, when Bonhoeffer, at the beginning of the church struggle, took a temporary position as pastor to two German-speaking congregations there. Bonhoeffer's motives in making this London move simply are not clear. Feil argues that Bonhoeffer really had no choice but to take the position in London since his forthright stand on the Jewish question involved a refusal to serve in any church (especially the Prussian church) that distinguished between Jewish and Gentile Christians.[97] Bethge, however, accents the troubled nature of the decision, coming as it did in the midst of the growing church crisis, and states that Bonhoeffer "in his search for the right decision tormented those around him almost as much as he tormented himself."[98] This being the case it is rather strange that Bonhoeffer did not consult Barth on the move and chose instead to inform him of the change only after having taken up his new duties in London. Bonhoeffer at the time had developed a very high personal regard for Barth,[99] and in the letter he wrote informing Barth about the move he indicated that he did not want to consult him beforehand because he felt that he would have to do whatever Barth advised.[100] In the letter to Barth he mentioned the point stressed above by Feil, but then went on to confess a lack of clear insight into his own motives. Bonhoeffer wrote in his letter: "If one is going to discover quite definite reasons for such decisions after the event, one of the strongest, I believe, was that I simply did not any longer feel up to the questions and demands which came to me."[101] He mentioned also his feeling of increasing isolation from his friends as a result of his radical opposition to the "Aryan clause," a pronouncement excluding pastors of Jewish background from church positions. Bonhoeffer stated further: "The danger of making a gesture at the present moment seemed to me greater than that of going off for some quietness, so off I went."[102] Bonhoeffer mentioned personal uncertainty after the church's rejection of his proposed Bethel Confession[103] and then concluded his letter by asking Barth for his "frank opinion on all this," indicating that he was prepared "even for a sharp word" concerning his decision.

The "sharp word" from Barth was almost a month in coming, but sharp it was. Barth declared that this was no time for Bonhoeffer to seek personal quietness: "Now, one can on no account play Elijah under the juniper tree or Jonah under the gourd, but must shoot from both barrels! What's the use of the praise you lavish on me—from the other side of the channel."[104] After asking Bonhoeffer why he wasn't in Berlin to help him in a confrontation with the Council of Brethren of the Pastors' Emergency League,[105] Barth imperiously declared: "I just will not allow you to put such a private tragedy on the stage [Bonhoeffer's "personal necessity"] in view of what is at stake for the German church today, as though there were not time afterwards, when if God wills we have got a little way out of this muddle again, for the study of the different complexes and inhibitions from which you suffer, as indeed others also must."[106] Barth pressed hard his objections to Bonhoeffer's London move: "With your splendid theological armoury and your upright German figure, should you not perhaps be almost a little ashamed at a man like Heinrich Vogel, who wizened and worked up as he is, is just always there waving his arms like a windmill and shouting 'Confession! Confession!', in his own way—in power or in weakness, that doesn't matter so much—actually giving his testimony."[107] Then, after virtually ordering Bonhoeffer to return to Berlin on the next ship—or at most the "ship after next"—Barth ended his lengthy rebuke with the words: "You will understand it (the letter as a whole) in the friendly spirit in which it is intended. If I were not so attached to you, I would not let fly at you in this way."[108]

It is not clear how Barth's letter struck Bonhoeffer. He clearly did not return to Berlin on "the next ship" or the "ship after next." During his London stay, however, Bonhoeffer did much in ecumenical circles to state the case for the Confessing Church in its opposition to the pro-Nazi administration of the established church.[109] However, it was not until April 1935 that Bonhoeffer returned to Germany to take on the responsibility of director of a pastors' seminary of the Confessing Church, a difficult decision for Bonhoeffer to make since it involved setting aside long-standing plans to go to India to spend time with Gandhi. Then a year and a half after his return to Germany, Bonhoeffer wrote Barth again —in September 1936. In that 1936 letter he mentions Barth's earlier rebuke: "Since you wrote to me in England that time I was to return by the next ship or failing that by the ship after next, you have heard nothing from me in person. I must ask you to excuse me for that. But the arrow did strike home! I think it really was the ship after next on which I came home."[110]

But this second exchange of letters with Barth was to be equally as distressing as the first. Bonhoeffer gave expression to a surprising sensitivity when he mentioned his disappointment at not being invited to take part in a collection of essays honoring Barth.[111] He spoke also of his work on a book about "the Sermon on the Mount and the Pauline doctrine of justification and sanctification" (*The Cost of Discipleship*). Also in describing his work at the Finkenwalde seminary, Bonhoeffer wrote:

> You can hardly imagine how empty, how completely burnt out most of the brothers are when they come to the seminary. Empty not only as regards theological insights and still more as regards knowledge of the Bible, but also as regards their personal life. On an open evening—the only one in which I shared [in 1931]—you once said very seriously to the students that you sometimes felt as though you would rather give up all lectures and instead pay a surprise visit on someone and ask him, like old Tholuck, "How goes it with your soul?" The need has not been met since then, not even by the Confessing Church. But there are very few who recognize this sort of work with young theologians as a task of the church and do something about it. And it is really what everyone is waiting for.[112]

After continuing further in this vein, Bonhoeffer then asked Barth, in the light of recent discussions about Lutheran and Reformed church union, to do a work on the substantive theological issues dividing the two Protestant groups. Bonhoeffer insisted that only Barth could perform such a service since "No one knows enough."[113]

Barth's reply was again a sharp one. He wrote to Bonhoeffer saying: "You could have written to me with a quiet conscience long ago, even if in the meanwhile you were describing some theological curves which did not run quite parallel to my own. What claim do I have on you, that you should owe me a solemn reckoning?"[114] And, after rather rebuking Bonhoeffer for his concern about the *Festschrift* (the collection of essays in honor of Barth), Barth addressed himself to the matter of Bonhoeffer's Finkenwalde program and its tendencies toward pietism:

> Unless I am mistaken, it was Rott who showed me this summer the advice on scriptural meditation which was adopted in your seminary. I read it carefully, but I can hardly say that I am very happy about it. I cannot go with the distinction in principle between theological work and devotional edification which is evident in this piece of writing and which I can also perceive from your letter. Furthermore, an almost indefinable odor of a monastic eros and pathos in the former writing disturbs me; true, it would represent a new possibility compared with previous experiences in this field, but at the moment I still have neither a positive feeling nor a use for it.[115]

Barth set aside also Bonhoeffer's suggestion of a book on the issues separating Lutheran and Reformed groups during the sixteenth and seventeenth centuries, but he ended his letter with warm regards and the assurance of "serious concern" in Bonhoeffer's work.

Again, one is not entirely sure how Bonhoeffer took this second critical letter from Barth.[116] It does not seem that Barth was as sensitive to Bonhoeffer's concerns as he might have been. At any rate it is the case that Bonhoeffer never again wrote to Barth. In an early correspondence with Erwin Sutz, Bonhoeffer seemed to have longed for some special relationship with Barth,[117] but the relationship never developed along the lines he had hoped for.

The description of Bonhoeffer's relationship to Barth, over and above the correspondence concerning the London trip, is important in that it sheds light on Bonhoeffer's troubled uncertainties and his efforts to find and make his own way. The question that finally comes to the fore is: did not Bonhoeffer in his second return from America in July of 1939 finally become his own man, so to speak?

Essential to answering this question is the realization that Bonhoeffer's departure from Germany for America in June of 1939 was a move initiated primarily by Bonhoeffer himself. As a result of fast-moving political developments, Bonhoeffer's age group faced conscription in May 1939. To avoid that distressing prospect—and consistent with his pacifism—Bonhoeffer sought help from his friends at home and overseas. With aid from well-placed family friends in the military and on the local conscription board, Bonhoeffer was allowed a temporary deferment and was given permission to go to England in March of 1939.[118] There he arranged for a conversation with Bishop Bell, seeking a way out of his predicament, while at the same time conferring about matters related to the German church situation. In a letter to Bell setting up the meeting, Bonhoeffer spoke of "leaving Germany sometime," then of his upcoming conscription and his anxiety over making a public show of his pacifism since such an action might discredit the Confessing Church. Bonhoeffer also wrote Bell: "I have been thinking of going to the Mission Field, not as an escape out of the situation, but because I wish to serve somewhere where service is really wanted."[119] No sure possibilities of overseas service came from the meeting with Bell,[120] but upon hearing of Reinhold Niebuhr's presence in England, Bonhoeffer visited him on April 3, 1939, and indicated his need to get out of Germany. Niebuhr wrote one letter back to America which went astray, and then on May 1 Niebuhr wrote urgently to Henry Smith Leiper of the Federal Council of Churches:

Bonhoeffer is due for military service in July and will refuse to serve. The [Council of Brethren] of the Confessing Church would like to have him evade the issue and at the same time tell American Christians about their situation. To get him out they need rather formal and formidable invitations from America. . . . Today I received word from Bonhoeffer saying that time was short. If he is to make necessary arrangements he ought to have a cable as well as a confirming letter. If you think well of the idea of inviting him would you send him a cable if this has not been done.[121]

There is no evidence that Bonhoeffer had in fact taken this whole matter up with the governing body of the Confessing Church prior to his visit to England and the conversations with Bell and Niebuhr. Bethge seems to indicate that the discussions with the Council came only later, when Bonhoeffer had the invitations in hand.[122] Ten days after the letter to Leiper, Niebuhr wrote Paul Lehmann asking him to help set up a lecture tour for Bonhoeffer and stating his understanding of Bonhoeffer's purpose: "He came to see me shortly upon our arrival and is anxious to come to America to evade for the time being a call to the colors. . . . There will be some difficulty in getting him out and if he fails he will land in prison."[123]

Bonhoeffer received the invitation to come to America, thus forestalling military induction. He then also sought and received permission from the Council of Brethren to go to America. With all clearances in hand Bonhoeffer left Berlin by air for London on June 2, 1939. After a short visit with the Leibholzes he joined his brother Karl-Friedrich on board the *Bremen* for the voyage to America, Karl-Friedrich having been invited to lecture at the University of Chicago.[124]

But the arrival in New York on June 12, far from bringing a sense of relief and new purpose, seemed only to deepen Bonhoeffer's uncertainty about his decision.[125] He was almost immediately confronted with the question of emigration.[126] He was dissatisfied with a proffered position with the Federal Council of Churches as chaplain to German refugees, fearing that such work might preclude a return to Germany. On the 17th of June he wrote to Lehmann underlining the point that he was *not* a refugee and that he would be returning to Germany in late fall or at the beginning of the new year. A diary he kept during this American visit notes homesickness, a desire to take the next ship home, awareness of having made a wrong decision.[127] He wrote to himself: "It is cowardice and weakness to run away here now."[128] And then on June 20th Bonhoeffer informed Dr. Henry Sloane Coffin, president of Union Theological Seminary, that he must go back to Germany, even though the diary indicates he remained confused about his motives in this new decision.[129] On the 26th of June he wrote: "We are just like soldiers who come away from the field on leave and despite everything that they expected are forced back there again. We cannot get away from it. Not as though we were necessary, as though we were needed (by God?!), but simply because our life is there and because we leave our life behind, we destroy it, if we are not back there. There is nothing pious about it, but something almost vital. But God acts not only through pious emotions, but also through these vital ones."[130] And the following day Bonhoeffer notes: "I wonder if the Americans do not understand us at all because they are people who left Europe so as to be able to live out their faith for themselves in freedom? i.e., because they did not stand fast by the last decision in the question of belief? I feel that they would understand the fugitive better than the one who stays. Hence the American tolerance, or rather, indifference in dogmatic questions. A warlike encounter is excluded, but so too is the true passionate longing for unity in faith."[131]

In a letter of explanation to Niebuhr, he stated his belief that he "made a mistake in coming to America" and asserted: "I will have no right to participate in the reconstruction of Christian life in Germany after the war if I do not share the trials of this time with my people. My brethren in the Confessing Synod wanted me to go. They may have been right in urging me to do so; but I was wrong in going. Such a decision each man must make for himself."[132] Bonhoeffer moved up the date of his return to Germany from August to July 8. On the eve of his departure from New York he wrote: "I am glad to have been over and glad that I am on the way home. Perhaps I have learnt more in this month than in a whole year nine years ago; at least I have acquired some important insight for all future decisions. Probably this visit will have a great effect on me."[133] And one day after his departure he wrote: "Since I have been on the ship my inner uncertainty about the future has ceased. I can think of my shortened time in America without reproaches."[134]

Bethge, in his appraisal of this sequence of events, makes use of the term "flight." The term is not inappropriate. The whole complex of moves attending Bonhoeffer's trip to America in 1939 was clearly engineered by Bonhoeffer himself; and serious reservations must be held regarding his statement in a letter to Leiper (June 15, 1939): "My personal question and difficulty with regard to military service, etc., came in only as a second consideration."[135] Bethge himself suggests that perhaps the letter to Bell (in March), requesting a meeting and citing his impending conscription, comes closest to the truth—but even that, Bethge says, "includes only a part of the whole."[136] One notes that his 1939 trip to London was set up before he actually secured from Hans Böhm of the Lutheran Union a commission of church business.[137] And he lingered on in England during March and April because he thought the war was about to break out and that being "caught" in England by such an eventuality would be a happy resolution of his problems.[138] It also seems evident, as already pointed out, that Bonhoeffer's discussions with the Council of Brethren about his trip to America came about *after* the invitations to visit America were in hand.[139] On this point, Bethge observes that in giving Bonhoeffer permission to go to America, "the Council of Brethren had never liked to refuse Bonhoeffer a wish."[140] Bethge, nonetheless, endeavors to give Bonhoeffer the benefit of the doubt in offering the following interpretation:

> To describe Bonhoeffer's travels of 1939 as "flight" is to use hindsight. He himself did not use the term, either to his friends—which of them knew the whole tangle of arguments and ought to have told him that to take such a step was an evasion?—or to his relatives, although they would have been delighted if it had been so and he had actually re-

mained abroad. For all that, he himself was by no means entirely clear about the crucial reasons for those journeys.[141]

At this point one is reminded of a trait in Bonhoeffer identified by Bethge—his tendency to plan carefully and "cover his moves" so to speak. In his 1935 departure from London to Germany to take up the duties of director of the pastors' seminary, Bonhoeffer made arrangements so that his departure from the London pastorates was understood only as a sabbatical leave, thus allowing for his return if things did not work out in Germany. Bethge observes: "Bonhoeffer so arranged his transfer from the pastorate to the seminary as not to preclude a possible return, a precaution *he never failed to take as long as circumstances allowed.*"[142] Bethge cites other instances of this sort of "careful provision" and then refers explicitly to the events of 1939: "When in 1939 he again proposed to strike out in a new direction, he exercised the same caution, but that was to be the last time, for subsequently he was to burn all his boats."[143] Bethge states that, with regard to the term "flight," Bonhoeffer never used this word himself, either to his friends or to his relatives. But Bonhoeffer came very close to such a description when he wrote in his American diary, "It is cowardice and weakness to run away here now."[144] And this, one may surmise, was really what all the "homesickness," all the "soul-searching" in America was about. This is also why he felt such relief when he finally decided to go back and why he was able to say on the eve before his voyage back to Germany: "Perhaps I have learnt more in this month than in a whole year nine years ago; at least I have acquired some important insight for all future decisions. Probably this visit will have a great effect on me."[145] It was not theological insight that made Bonhoeffer's month in America noteworthy[146] but his own confrontation with himself. Completely on his own, Bonhoeffer had taken, if not the next ship back home, the ship after next.

THE IMPACT OF THE CRISIS

Many of those who have argued for the essential continuity of Bonhoeffer's thought have emphasized the passage in the prison letters in which Bonhoeffer, writing to Bethge, declares: "I don't think I've ever changed very much, except perhaps at the time of my first impressions abroad and under the first conscious influence of father's personality. . . . Self-development is, of course, a different matter. Neither of us has really had a break in our lives. Of course, we have deliberately broken with a good deal, but that again is something quite different. . . . I sometimes used to long for something of the kind, but today I think differently about it. Continuity with one's own past is a great gift, too."[147] Bonhoeffer here sees his life as one of essential continuity but strangely leaves out of question the matter of "self-development." He notes that for a while he longed for a radical break in his life; and one cannot help but identify this as a reference to the heroic spirituality of *The Cost of Discipleship*. On the face of it the statement is not enough to discount the special significance of the return from America, especially since Bonhoeffer seems to have regarded that event as a step in his self-development and retrospectively viewed it as evidence of who and what he was all along. In the light of his claim of no breaks in his life, it is important to note that in the letter immediately preceding the one in which he makes that claim, Bonhoeffer takes note of a fellow prisoner who felt that his last years were completely wasted. Bonhoeffer comments: "I'm glad that I have never yet had that feeling even for a moment. Nor have I ever regretted my decision in the summer of 1939, for I'm firmly convinced— however strange it may seem—that my life has followed a straight and unbroken course, at any rate in its outward conduct."[148] And again in the letter of December 22, 1943, Bonhoeffer wrote to Bethge:

> Now I want to assure you that I haven't for a moment regretted coming back in 1939—nor any of the consequences, either. I knew quite well

what I was doing, and I acted with a clear conscience. I've no wish to cross out of my life anything that has happened since, either to me personally (would I have gotten engaged otherwise? would you have married? Sigurdshof, East Prussia, Ettal, my illness and all the help you gave me then, and the time in Berlin), or as regards events in general. And I regard my being kept here . . . as being involved in Germany's fate, as I was resolved to be. I don't look back on the past and accept the present reproachfully, but I don't want the machinations of men to make me waver.[149]

Here, it appears, Bonhoeffer viewed his life from the time of that crucial 1939 decision as all of a piece—and that he regarded his later imprisonment as simply an aspect of his "resolve" to be "involved in Germany's fate."

A weighing of these references—and Bonhoeffer in prison refers to no event in his life as he does to the 1939 decision—certainly suggests a special significance for the decision to return from America on the eve of World War II. We have seen how he spoke in his American diary of his decision to return to Germany, and of his feeling that, like a soldier on leave from the field, he is forced to return: *"There is nothing pious about it, but something almost vital. But God acts not only through pious emotions, but also through these vital ones."*[150] Here it is not too much to say, I think, that an end is written to *The Cost of Discipleship*—and was this not in fact a break? Events and the question, "Who am I?" had caught up with him and a time of final decision had come. It is not surprising that the practice of personal confession should hereafter fall by the way.[151] Nor is it surprising that the prime ethical category should now become "responsibility" rather than "obedience."

What happens from this point on is that the largely latent strength/weakness motif comes increasingly to the fore. "God acts not only through pious emotions, but also through these vital ones"; or, as he put it later in *Ethics,* "Being loved by God does not by any means deprive man of his mighty thoughts and his spirited deeds."[152] Bonhoeffer's personal, existential decision—and no longer the logic of Barth's struggle against natural theology and idolatry—comes to play the dominant role in the structuring of Bonhoeffer's theology.

Take for example the (previously quoted) entry in Bonhoeffer's diary seven days after his decision to return to Germany: "I wonder if the Americans do not understand us at all because they are people who left Europe so as to be able to live out their faith for themselves in freedom? i.e., because they did not stand fast by the last decision [i.e., death] in the question of belief? . . . Hence the American tolerance, or rather, indifference in dogmatic questions. A warlike encounter is excluded, but so too is the true passionate longing for unity in faith."[153] In an essay begun at Union Theological Seminary and completed later in Europe, Bonhoeffer expands this thought and makes it the major content of his discussion of American Christianity, "Protestantism Without Reformation."[154] In effect he reads the history of American Christianity in the light of his own experience of being briefly a refugee and then his decision to risk everything by returning home.

As Bonhoeffer saw in American Christianity an unwillingness to "stand fast by the last decision in the question of belief," so thoughts about death came increasingly to the fore in the subsequent months. After Bonhoeffer's return to Germany, Niebuhr recommended him to John Baillie as a possible candidate for the Croall Lectures at the University of Edinburgh. Invited by Baillie to undertake these lectures, Bonhoeffer accepted and suggested the title, "Death in the Christian Message."[155] A theme of Bonhoeffer's first circular letter to the Finkenwalde seminarians after his return —and after the outbreak of war—was the distinction between a "death from outside" and a "death in us." Bonhoeffer in this circular letter speaks rather strangely of the "dying within" as coming from the fall of Adam and says: "This death is grace and the consummation of love . . . ; our death is really only the way to the perfect love of God."[156] And Bethge offers a further statement of this matter:

> Just after the First World War, when he was fourteen, he [took]
> . . . with him from an exhibition of Max Klinger's work a reproduction

of the lithograph *Vom Tode.* Later he could remark, as if incidentally, that he expected an early death. Now, at the beginning of the Second World War . . . Bonhoeffer was . . . beginning, too, to take a literary interest in the theme of death, for example, in the works of Joachim Wach, Fritz Dehn, and Georges Barbarin.[157]

One has seriously to ask, in terms of Bonhoeffer's later work, whether the anthropological question, shaded strongly by Bonhoeffer's own experience, does not come to represent the real center of gravity? True, in sections of the *Ethics* there is a lingering on of the Christocentric logic of Barth, especially in connection with the theme of the mandates. But in the development of Bonhoeffer's other major new concepts in *Ethics,* the relation of the ultimate and the penultimate, the anthropological starting point is obvious and justification by faith is, as it were, projected into the future to become operative at the time of death. Justification takes up into itself, at the end, the whole of the vital and the "natural":

> But the justifying word of God is also a final word in the sense of time. It is always preceded by something penultimate, some action, suffering, movement, volition, defeat, uprising, entreaty or hope, that is to say, in a quite genuine sense by a span of time, at the end of which it stands. *Only he can be justified who has already become the object of an accusation in time.* Justification presupposes that the creature has incurred guilt. . . . A way must be traversed, even though, in fact, there is no way that leads to this goal, this way must be pursued to the end, that is to say, to the point at which God sets an end to it.[158]

Following these lines of argument, it is not really surprising that death, and the acceptance of death, should become in the prison letters a clue to the proper understanding of the Old Testament. Whereas once—at Finkenwalde and in the thought of *The Cost of Discipleship*—Christ was the only clue to the reading of the Old Testament, Bonhoeffer subsequently complains that "we still read the New Testament far too little in the light of the Old."[159] Is it really surprising that the world come of age becomes the basic reality of those later letters and that Christology becomes a question? If the *deus ex machina* can be construed as a projection from the situation of human weakness and need, certainly the implied criticism of a God who stoops to weakness can be viewed as an extension of the experience of human strength. The only thing that is really surprising in all of this is that the generally careful and creditable scholarship of Feil should conclude—without hesitation —that "the world come of age is grounded not biographically in Bonhoeffer's personal development, but historically in a profound change of the times." At this point, we are drawn rather to agree with the observation of Ott, who says of Bonhoeffer's postulate of a nonreligious interpretation of Christianity: "Surely . . . this postulate has been nourished at other springs. . . . Behind it are other motives, another and much stronger foundation, than merely a certain theoretical judgment on the course of history."[160]

We have previously noted that interpretations of Bonhoeffer are more or less convincing depending on their capacity to treat adequately the variety of themes and shifting accents that are to be found in his collected writings. That judgment is to be applied to this analysis as well. What cannot be done, I think, is—amid all of Bonhoeffer's admitted Christocentrism—to allow the ever-present strength/weakness theme to be treated as a benign incidental, lacking in theological import or existential "concreteness."

∾ 6 ∾

The Nature
of the Dissent

This study is not intended to diminish Bonhoeffer's witness of faith. In a very special way the worldwide Christian community has garnered strength from Bonhoeffer's steadfast concern for Christ, and certainly his perseverance in faith will continue to sustain others. There were, of course, other Christians who made a similar witness and about whom we know less; but our indebtedness reaches out through Bonhoeffer to them as well.

QUEST AND COHERENCE

The point, however, that emerges from this analysis is that Bonhoeffer's discipleship was also a quest, and this had important theological implications. Bold Christological affirmations yielded at some points to questions. "Reality" for Bonhoeffer bore a certain flux that was not so much a reflection of "the nature of things" as a mark of his own search for certainty. At one stage this quest was informed by obedience and monastic rigor; later, faith was defined by living wholly in this world. This turn of the quest is a result in part of the pressure of external events: time would no longer wait for a spiritual "sign," and a decision for integrity had to be made. Bonhoeffer reached out and affirmed a human possibility that has always been a part of the Western tradition—one that all along bore a strong attraction for him. What is striking about Bonhoeffer's testimony is that this possibility, which stands independent of faith, was to be claimed for faith, and "man come of age" was to be also *Christian* man.

Gerhard Ebeling, in one of the earliest major analyses of Bonhoeffer's thought, stated: "The basic structure of 'religion' is the supplementing of reality by God. That could, I think, be taken as the common denominator of all the many different things Bonhoeffer says about religion. . . ."[1] Bonhoeffer, as Ebeling sees it, was opposed to "religion," i.e., "the thinking in terms of two spheres . . . , striving to make room for God, understanding transcendence in the epistemological and metaphysical sense or in the sense of what surpasses the possibilities of man, localizing the experience of transcendence on the boundaries of existence, treating it schematically as the solution of unsolved problems, God's role as a 'stopgap,' spying out and exploiting man's weaknesses as proof of his need of God, the view that being a Christian is a special kind of existence, shifting the emphasis on to an individualistic view of salvation, on to inwardness or into the Beyond. . . ."[2] Yes, we nod —this is all part of "religion" and this was what Bonhoeffer was opposed to. Yet, if we allow Ebeling's understanding to stand, on a more fundamental level Bonhoeffer was also a "religious man" —in spite of all his protests. On the anthropological level there is a sense in which Bonhoeffer's attempt to claim "man come of age" as "Christian man" was a "religious" effort, a supplementing of an independent reality with God.

In one of his prison letters Bonhoeffer deplored the "fatal leap" back into the Middle Ages. He viewed this as an effort on the part of many Christians to escape back into a "world of God."[3] Surely the Middle Ages was a religious period, an age of metaphysics that "supplemented reality with God" and also added to the cardinal virtues of man (justice, courage, wisdom, temperance) the theological virtues (faith, hope, and charity). And yet in his own way Bonhoeffer also was working at this task. Bonhoeffer wanted to add faith, hope, and charity to a basic human reality. Bonhoeffer gave expression to the "religious" longing for Christendom—a kind of medieval longing—an attraction for the "both/and."

After his decision to return to Germany in 1939, Bonhoeffer suggested that American Christianity lacked a feeling for "the last decision in the question of belief," and therefore lacked also *"the true passionate longing for unity in faith."* The desire for synthesis —inspired no doubt by his family background, his cultural heritage —is a traceable motif in Bonhoeffer's thought, despite polemical tendencies on behalf of the Barthian logic of revelation. In *The Communion of Saints* the longing for unity combined sociology and theology; shortly thereafter it balanced "Act" and "Being"; in *The Cost of Discipleship* it merged faith and works; in *Ethics* it eliminated the "two spheres"; and in the prison letters "man come of age" was to be also "Christian man."

These patterns of synthetic thinking reflect Bonhoeffer's uncertain anthropology. Bonhoeffer seemed to fear that the bold deed which alone "can strike at the heart of evil and overcome it" (*Ethics*), would somehow be ruled out by piety. In the prison letters the earlier challenge of "confessionalism" loses much of its allure and becomes instead a "law of faith," a bulwark of clericalism.[4] Barth's achievement was later characterized as a "positivism of revelation" leading on to a "conservative restoration."[5] In the letters, after reading W. F. Otto's study of the Greek gods and being impressed by that "world of faith, which sprang from the wealth and depth of human existence, not from its cares and longings," Bonhoeffer felt that he could almost "claim these gods for Christ."[6] The idea of a *cantus firmus* that held together the other varied melodies of life likewise bore the impulse of synthesis.[7] And both "resistance" and "submission" were to be given their due in life.[8]

The matter of Bonhoeffer's personal quest, his longing for an answer to the question "Who am I?", the pull of his family and his own liberal heritage, the synthetic impulse, his fascination with the heroic: these uniquely personal, existential concerns make Bonhoeffer's theology something less than systematic. There is clearly a Christological concern in Bonhoeffer's thinking, but it does not always play the formative role; and it cannot be accorded the weight that so many of his interpreters have tried to give it. His varied Christological statements are not to be understood independently of his anxious wrestling with the question of his own faith. To put it another way, the "Christ for others" does not consistently mirror a "Christ for me," and thus it can at points be interpreted as suggesting a certain *noblesse oblige*. In short, despite Bonhoeffer's persistent attacks upon inwardness and individualism, his own thought is severely disturbed by these same tendencies. And one must here note that Bonhoeffer frequently attacked patterns of life and thought that were at times profoundly his own. Thus he spoke out forcefully against the "imitation of Christ," yet he himself seemed strongly drawn to this form of the spiritual life. Although he vigorously attacked inwardness and piety, he also complained in his "Outline for a Book" that Barth and the Confessing Church "have encouraged us to entrench ourselves persistently behind the 'faith of the Church' and evade the honest question as to what we ourselves really believe."[9]

These criticisms weigh heavily against the systematic coherence of Bonhoeffer's work and impel agreement with the early judgment that there was an impulsive tendency in Bonhoeffer's theological efforts. Here we are saying that Bonhoeffer's own deep involvement in the struggle of faith, its constant presence in his life, its anxious character, work against a reasoned and fully coherent theological statement. Bonhoeffer, in his theological work at least, never seemed to arrive at that point of freedom which might have allowed him to "boast in his weaknesses" and to stand off from "his shipwrecks, his beatings, his dangers" (II Cor., chs. 11 and 12). Was it not the urgency of the anthropological question, the suggestion that "faith" somehow had to become real for him, that led Bonhoeffer on from one position to another? Perhaps the times dictated such movement—buy why in the end should the world's "coming-of-age" have been taken so seriously? Perhaps the accepted norms of "maturity," "manhood," "womanhood," are simply not of great importance in the context of grace. And perhaps a Christian *hilaritas* is something apart from self-possession.[10]

HISTORICAL PERCEPTION

In addition, however, one has to deal with a second dimension of Bonhoeffer's thought, a dimension that has strong bearing on the claim of "epochal status" often made in relation to his later theological formulations. Here one is called to point out Bonhoeffer's rather limited involvement in the crucial events of the century. Such an observation, or assertion, may appear to be wrongheaded and to be flying in the face of the facts. It may be pointed out that almost no theologian in modern times was as deeply involved in events as was Bonhoeffer. Yet one must note a peculiar feature to Bonhoeffer's life: it falls somehow "between the times." Bonhoeffer was, in his own view, "too young" to know the full reality of World War I; and despite some attempts at prophetic vision he was never able to weigh the totality of World War II, the event that consumed his own life.

Bonhoeffer very early spoke of his noninvolvement in World War I, or at least marked off his own historical experience from those who had actually fought in the war. In his February 1933 radio speech on the theme of the "leadership principle," a speech that was cut off the air before its completion,[11] Bonhoeffer noted a difference between three age groups within the younger generation of Germany. He declared:

> Three brothers, of whom the eldest was born in 1900, the second in 1905 and the third in 1910, who are thus now 33, 28, and 23 respectively, today embody three different generations. Yet they all belong to what is usually called "the younger generation"; the eldest came to intellectual maturity while the war was still on, the second under the influence of the years after the collapse, and the third in the years of an age which we cannot yet describe, shall we say since 1926. The speed of historical events has accelerated the rate of change of generations almost tenfold. . . . We must speak of a change of generation when a group of young men of the same age together refer to an event characteristic of their whole spiritual and intellectual attitude and feel them-

selves to be . . . an independent group rooted in this special unity of experience.[12]

Bonhoeffer, of course, belonged to the second age group, not the first. And he clearly set himself apart from the generation that fought World War I. The terms in which he described the war generation are especially important, for they express a sense of isolation and non-participation on Bonhoeffer's part. The statement is worth quoting at some length. "The first group," Bonhoeffer says,

> is of men who have seen death, who have as it were daily emerged afresh from death to life, who have come to know life as risk and gain and who therefore still command a quite peculiar breadth of thought. They have an attitude of almost destructive hardness towards their own lives and the lives of others and yet also a strong affirmation of life and responsibility for the lives of others. This generation of young warriors presents closed ranks to its younger brothers. Its whole attitude, consciously or not, is an expression of inaccessible superiority over those younger than itself; there is something like scorn on the faces of these men, marked by life and death, scorn at those who are completely inexperienced, who live without knowing what life really means. There is an invisible but impenetrable line dividing those who were in the war from those, only slightly younger, who grew up and became mature at the time of the collapse [Bonhoeffer's group]. This is felt more strongly by the younger men than by the older ones. For the first post-war generation there is nothing more impressive than the fact that there in their midst and alongside them are these men alive, who have escaped from the world of death. There is something worrying, disquieting, terrifying in this recognition.[13]

What is striking about this description—along with Bonhoeffer's strong sense of exclusion—is the manner in which Bonhoeffer viewed the historical experience of the war generation. They are those who have faced death and know what life is all about; they display "scorn at those who are completely inexperienced"; they convey an attitude of "inaccessible superiority." These are the terms of the heroic and the individualistic. They say little of the crisis of meaning which, culturally speaking, World War I also represents. Bonhoeffer not only admits to isolation from the experience of World War I; but in 1933 he reveals no searching grasp of the war's larger historical meaning.[14] This fact is not only a feature of this particular lecture but is generally characteristic of what Bonhoeffer had to say about World War I up to that time.[15]

What Bonhoeffer says about his relationship to the event of World War I must in a slightly different sense be said also about his understanding of World War II. Bonhoeffer's struggle in World War II was, like that of many others, a struggle against the Nazis. But he, with others, is a special case in that he fought against the currents of nationalism and conceived of the major issue as nothing less than the survival of civilization itself. In the course of the struggle, however, when he entertained thoughts about a new order, there are hints again of the heroic, aristocratic ethos that subtly shaped his expectations. In some "thoughts" on the occasion of the baptism of Bethge's son, Bonhoeffer wrote:

> [There is a] question whether we are moving towards an age of the selection of the fittest, i.e., an aristocratic society, or to uniformity in all material and spiritual aspects of human life. Although there has been a very far-reaching equalisation here, the sensitiveness in all ranks of society for the human values of justice, achievement, and courage could create a new selection of people who will be allowed the right to provide strong leadership. It will not be difficult for us to renounce our privileges, recognizing the justice of history. We may have to face events and changes that take no account of our wishes and our rights. But if so, we shall not give way to embittered and barren pride, but consciously submit to divine judgment, and so prove ourselves worthy to survive by identifying ourselves generously and unselfishly with the life of the community and the sufferings of our fellowmen.[16]

In these words about giving up privileges, avoiding "embittered pride," proving "ourselves worthy to survive by identifying ourselves generously and unselfishly with the life of the community and the sufferings of our fellowmen," there is lacking that troubled sense of defeat which came even to the victors after the war. The situation that followed the war—the impasse of cold war, the sudden rebirth of hatred and fear—seemed to make a mockery of human hope and the terrible sacrifices that were made. Only the unbelievable extent of the Nazi horror spoke to the necessity of the sacrifice. Despite his own special knowledge of the Nazi threat to civilization, Bonhoeffer really did not know the event of World War II in its entirety.

At issue in the matter of Bonhoeffer's abridged perspective on World War II is once more the question of anthropology. What occurred intellectually and spiritually after the war was an explosion of the existentialist point of view. The French existentialists, especially Sartre and Camus, writing out of the situation of France's defeat, discovered that they had a world audience. And in the surge of postwar interest in existentialism, there is discernible a deep-rooted awareness of the problem of meaning in history. Thus not only the "ultimate" (and individualistic) questions of death, self-awareness, and alienation but also the defeat of corporate purpose constituted an integral dimension of post–World War II existentialism. Bonhoeffer knew little of this historical crisis of meaning, which stands as an important dimension of the total event of World War II, and thus to read Bonhoeffer's polemics against existentialism in the prison letters is to realize how restricted in some ways was his view of World War II. In the prison letters we have not the assimilation and transcendence of a crucial world event but its premature assessment. Similarly, with regard to Bonhoeffer's views of existentialism we must say that his understanding of that phenomenon was severely limited by its Kierkegaardian and theological form, with little awareness of its grounding in a social, corporate experience. One of the ironies of a later effort to elaborate Bonhoeffer's thought (Cox's *The Secular City*) is that Albert Camus, who understood better than many other existentialists the pathos of man's historical experience, is somehow made a model of "man come of age."[17]

To sum up this aspect of Bonhoeffer's thought, one must say that not only did Bonhoeffer start off his theological work with a restricted, limited understanding of World War I; in his later thought he reflects an abridged and deficient assessment of World

War II. It is thus not surprising that Bonhoeffer's vision of the future was tinged with a certain *noblesse oblige.* There is some mellowing and softening of the hard heroic of *The Cost of Discipleship,* but *in toto* Bonhoeffer's grasp of historical reality hardly bespeaks an "epochal" point of view. Despite all that Bonhoeffer had to say against individualism and inwardness, he seems not to have arisen, at this point, above his own involvements. This really is not to fault Bonhoeffer: it reminds us of who he was and what he gave of himself. But it certainly should caution restraint in appraisal of Bonhoeffer's theological significance.

ANTHROPOLOGY AND
BIBLICAL HERMENEUTICS

In the final instance, rather than providing us with enduring new theological conceptions, Bonhoeffer helps to bring to the surface a persistent and nagging question: the question of a theological anthropology and its role in hermeneutics. Bonhoeffer does not move beyond this problem but is himself deeply immersed in it. For example, all of the discussion of what Bonhoeffer may have implied in his aphorism "the positivism of revelation" has not brought clarity on this point. Certainly a major aspect of his meaning was Bonhoeffer's own unsatisfying pursuit of the "logic" of revelation, the rejection of all natural theology, and the attribution of total reality to the Christ event. But later in rejecting what he felt to be a growing "law of faith" in the theology of Barth and the Confessing Church,[18] Bonhoeffer raised again the question of revelation and possible sources of revelation outside the Biblical witness. A suggestion of this movement is to be found in his later interest in an "unconscious Christianity," which he seemed on the point of elaborating.[19] While one can agree with Bethge that the concept of a "secret discipline" indicates that Bonhoeffer did not intend to abandon ecclesiology and the corporate forms of faith, still one is impressed more with the inner tensions that emerge from his fragmentary theological statements than with the direction that they clearly chart.

To put the matter differently: what weight is to be given to Bonhoeffer's "sociocultural" description of a "world come of age" in the interpretation of the Biblical material? Bonhoeffer's most forceful statement of this hypothesis, i.e., the "world come of age," appears in his attacks on "religion" (defined to a large degree by means of the strength/weakness contrast) and the history of Christian apologetics. But Bonhoeffer has much greater difficulty moving from this sphere of historical-theological criticism to an exposition of the Biblical materials themselves (the question of the "non-religious interpretation of biblical concepts"). The one firm footing that Bonhoeffer *seems* to achieve in this area is his renewed appreciation for the "this-worldliness" of the Old Testament and his insistence that the New Testament must be read more in the light of the Old. Here the apparent deemphasis of the problem of death in the Old Testament figures large in Bonhoeffer's reevaluation of the Old Testament Scriptures and appears to offer support for reading the Biblical materials in the light of the image of "man come of age." But try as he might, Bonhoeffer did not get very far with his "non-religious interpretation." And in his letters to Bethge it is the question that is constantly being put off, a matter to which more thought had always to be given.[20]

Here one can suggest that Bonhoeffer's project ran into difficulties because he was attempting to use a certain anthropology and image ("man come of age") to interpret materials which in fact do not sustain the hypothesis. Rather, the Biblical materials, more than anything else, stand athwart any anthropology that finds man's essential being in his competence, his strength, his ability to cope with reality. In the original correspondence, Bethge raised a crucial point when he asked Bonhoeffer the disarming question "whether Jesus didn't use men's 'distress' as a point of contact with them, and whether therefore the 'methodism' that [Bonhoeffer] criticized earlier isn't right."[21] The point that Bethge was making was that the New Testament materials do not in the least suggest that persons are any less persons for the presence in their lives of need, sin, and weakness; and that actually Jesus' ministry seems to have been addressed in a very special way to these persons. In this context, one is reminded of the saying of Jesus: "Those who are well have no need of a physician, but those who are sick; I have not come to call the righteous, but sinners to repentance."[22] Here one must simply say that Bonhoeffer was off the mark when he commented, "It is weakness rather than wickedness that perverts a man and drags him down and it needs profound sympathy to put up with that."[23] The same is true of Bonhoeffer's suggestion that "people's weakness (stupidity, lack of independence, forgetfulness, cowardice, vanity, corruptibility, temptability, etc.) [is] a greater danger than evil."[24]

Bonhoeffer at a later point seems to have attempted a further answer to Bethge's question. In the letter of June 30, 1944, Bonhoeffer wrote:

> When Jesus blessed sinners, they were real sinners, but Jesus did not make everyone a sinner first. He called them away from their sin, not into their sin. It is true that encounter with Jesus meant the reversal of all human values. So it was in the conversion of Paul, though in his case the encounter with Jesus preceded the realization of sin. It is true that Jesus cared about people on the fringe of human society, such as harlots and tax-collectors, but never about them alone, for he sought to care about man as such. Never did he question a man's health, vigour, or happiness, regarded in themselves, or regard them as evil fruits; else why should he heal the sick and restore strength to the weak? Jesus claims for himself and the Kingdom of God the whole of human life in all its manifestations.[25]

But this too is not really an answer to Bethge's question. It goes without saying that Jesus and the Biblical writers in general do not speak of health and goodness as evil, and that Jesus did not call men "into their sin"; this should never really be an issue. It has become an issue for Bonhoeffer because he has allowed his justifiable polemic against a certain type of "religiousness"—the "methodism" of those who prey upon "man's weakness for purposes that are alien to him"[26]—subtly to merge itself with the ideology of strength and vigor. The "importunity" of the existentialists and psychotherapists, Bonhoeffer declares, is "far too *unaristocratic* for the Word of God to ally itself with them. The Word of God is far removed from this revolt of mistrust, this revolt from below. On the contrary, it reigns."[27] Confusion has entered in and false antitheses are stated because Bonhoeffer has reached out to an aristocratic ideal to combat what he feels is common and mean within the "religious" tradition. The end result is that Bonhoeffer attempts to transpose the gospel into an aristocratic idiom even though the gospel cannot be read in that fashion.

And this, it should be noted, is true also for the Old Testament. No more than the New Testament can the Hebrew Scriptures be read as support for the "man come of age" image. As one commentator has pointed out (almost *too* simplistically), regarding Bonhoeffer's rejection of the idea of God as "problem-solver" and "need-fulfiller": "This stance is quite unbiblical. Surely the faith of Israel and the hope of the new Israel lie in a God who controls the fate of men and nations, answers the prayers of his people and intervenes to effect his will. But more important, just as the legitimization of the prophetic word was the fulfillment of prophecy so the intervention of God was in fact the very *ground* of belief in God."[28] As for the claim that something is "far too *unaristocratic* for the Word of God to ally itself with," it is hard, I think, to conceive of a tradition more inimical to the aristocratic motif than the Biblical.[29]

At one point in the prison letters, Bonhoeffer speculated about the fate and form of Christianity in a religionless world. He suggested that the time of "religion" had passed, that nineteen hundred years of Christian preaching rests upon the supposition of the "religious a priori." With this—his own supposition concerning the coming-of-age of the world—Bonhoeffer opened a breach with the Biblical world of faith. He was unable to close that breach with his 'non-religious interpretation of biblical concepts." Apparently he did not see that the Bible opens its own breach in the realm of anthropology.

It is not clear, however, that Bonhoeffer finally settled for "man come of age" and "religionless" Christianity. The persistence of the question, "Who am I?" carried through even his most assertive and provocative letters. And when in his last letters to Bethge he spoke again of the nature of his faith, his words are startlingly familiar:[30]

> God does not give us everything we want, but he does fulfil all his promises, i.e. . . . he preserves his church, constantly renewing our faith and not laying on us more than we can bear, gladdening us with his nearness and help, hearing our prayers, and leading us along the best and straightest paths to himself.[31]

He also writes: "I've often found it a great help to think in the evening of all those who I know are praying for me, children as well as grownups. I think I owe it to the prayers of others, both known and unknown, that I have often been kept in safety."[32] And in his very last letter to Bethge, he wrote:

> I am so sure of God's guiding hand that I hope I shall always be kept in that certainty. You must never doubt that I'm travelling with gratitude and cheerfulness along the road where I'm being led. My past life is brim-full of God's goodness, and my sins are covered by the forgiving love of Christ crucified. I'm most thankful for the people I have met, and I only hope that they never have to grieve about me, but that they, too, will always be certain of, and thankful for, God's mercy and forgiveness.[33]

At the end, Bonhoeffer's statement of faith and his humanity were not very different from the faith and humanity of the long nineteen hundred years of Christian history. And it is this Bonhoeffer—not the restless, provocative theologian—who is likely to strengthen and nurture the faith of the church.

Epilogue

If a simplification is to be made of this analysis, it is the following: not Christology, but anthropology represents the spur of Bonhoeffer's later thought. Such a conclusion underlines the basic nature of anthropology in the framing of theological statements. It is by no means a novel or surprising conclusion since this is a generalization that can be applied to much of the theology that has been written over the last two hundred years.

John Calvin, in the sixteenth century, insisted that the knowledge of God and the knowledge of man are interrelated. But the starting point in Calvin's perception was the reality of God.[1] Subsequently the starting point was to be fixed more and more in man, a development to which, as has been pointed out, the Lutheran doctrine of *finitum capax infiniti* may have significantly contributed.[2] In the latter half of the eighteenth century and also in the nineteenth century, liberal theology approached the question of God no longer through a historical witness, a Biblical record, but chiefly through the human faculty of "conscience" or "feeling." And subsequently Feuerbach, at least in Barth's view, gave the "show" away when he pursued this logic to its end and insisted that "God" was really an expression of man's idealized image of himself. Freud's variation on Feuerbach was that "God" was simply a fanciful projection of man's need, a sublime father image.

Barth's role in this brief résumé of theological history was his effort to call a halt to this exaggerated emphasis on man within the theological tradition, an emphasis that clearly reflected the presuppositions of the culture at large. His first attempt in this regard was to insist on the "otherness" of God, the objective character of revelation, and the Scriptural witness to Christ. He also challenged the apotheosis of man with a forceful reassertion of the doctrine of sin. But outside of this latter point, Barth came only gradually to a full-fledged discussion of anthropology and rather late to a positive statement in this regard. Through almost three decades (1920–1950) the accent—perhaps understandably, in the light of the needed corrective and the realities of the historical situation—fell upon the sovereignty of God, and God's gracious act in Christ. It was not until the 1950's that Barth's word about man came more clearly to the fore.[3]

The theological problem that all of this raises in the light of an analysis of Bonhoeffer is that, at least for Bonhoeffer, Barth's earlier theological corrective was not sufficient. Bonhoeffer had a compulsion to work at the anthropological question—and personally sought an answer here. Thus despite Bonhoeffer's formal "Barthian" course up through portions of the *Ethics,* and despite his Christocentric marking of the helm, the anthropological baggage lay loose in the hold and its shifting weight contributed to significant theological drift. In his letter to Barth in 1936, making reference to Tholuck and to his own work on *The Cost of Discipleship,* Bonhoeffer forthrightly stated his anthropological involvement. And Barth's "pastoral" failure at this point may well have worked against Barth's own theological purposes. At any rate, the anthropological question was not contained by Bonhoeffer's studied Christocentrism—with the result that a Biblically alien anthropology came to command a new course.

An anthropological silence simply will not suffice. The question of man is the chief question for the world; and, although it is not the only question for theology, it certainly is there to be asked and answered alongside the questions about God, Christ,[4] and the world. Concern for the anthropological question should not and cannot be held off. And if at times theology has been hurt by its dominance, in actuality it is something of a two-edged sword. If the charge can be made against theology (and there is no reason why theology should not take the charge seriously) that anthropology shades and colors the talk about God, certainly theology can and should talk also about a humanity that is "shaded" and "colored" by God[5]—whether or not the world wants to consider the reality of God.

Barth was too restrictive at this point; he felt that a theological anthropology was viable only if "along the whole line the relation to God is one that is in principle uninvertible";[6] that is, one must frame an anthropology that cannot possibly lead to a confusion of man with "God." To have this as an understanding within the community of faith may have merit, but if Barth meant this to hold true also for an understanding from "without," as in the case of Feuerbach, it would seem to represent a subtle surrender to unfaith. Bultmann observed—and rightly so—that "faith, speaking of God as acting, cannot defend itself against the charge of being an illusion . . . [nor against the charge that it is simply] a psychologically subjective event."[7] The possibility will always exist that the observer of the man of faith will conclude that the God to whom that man bears witness is a projection of his needs and fancies. Here, too often, theology has become defensive and left all to "defend" God, thus allowing some anthropological "certainty" to secure the field. In fact, however, there are no anthropological certainties. The world's "maturity" is not necessarily the "maturity of faith," and this is reason enough to work at a theological anthropology. Bonhoeffer really did not do this; rather he tried to baptize the nearest anthropology by means of an "unconscious Christianity" and an "implicit faith."[8] By contrast, in the Old Testament story of David and the ark of the covenant (II Sam., ch. 6), Michal, David's wife, saw an "alien" humanity in David; and the thought should be pursued in connection with the New Testament that the "offense of the cross" might involve not only a "humiliated" deity but a "strange" humanity. Despite Luther's insight into the one, "the hiddenness of God," we have to ask whether he was not—with

his *"finitum capax infiniti"*—strangely blind to the other. Kierkegaard was much more insightful and suggestive here when in *Fear
and Trembling* he wrote: "The courage of faith is the only humble
courage."[9]

If, in the first instance, this analysis of Bonhoeffer has suggested
that theology ought properly to spend more—not less—time on the
anthropological question, a second point follows closely upon this.
Theology, no less than other disciplines which purport to take *man*
seriously, ought also to take *history* seriously; for history bears
anthropologies in its train. History is a testing of the hopes and
affirmations about man—and events have much to say about the
viability and currency of anthropologies.

In this regard Bonhoeffer's theology affords us surprisingly less
help than supposed. Bonhoeffer, as suggested in this analysis, lived
"between" the two most formative events of the twentieth century.
He did not live *through* them. He felt cut off from World War I
and, in its aftermath, confessed to feeling as though events had
passed him by.[10] This need not have been the case—but for Bonhoeffer it was. And this historical feeling may well have engendered
in Bonhoeffer the pressing urge to be his own man: in choosing
theology as a vocation, in trips abroad, in siding with Barth against
the liberal theology of Berlin, in early joining the struggle against
the German Christians and the Nazis, in affirming the "world
come of age," and in asserting his own "theological advance"
beyond Barth, Bultmann, *et al.* We do not propose this as some
sort of psychological analysis of Bonhoeffer, but offer it only to
suggest that without a grasp of the sociocultural meaning of World
War I, and without its due assimilation to a theological perspective,
Bonhoeffer's thought was prone to a romantic anthropological
statement.

In relation to World War I and World War II, in neither case
do we have in Bonhoeffer a grasp of the totality of an "event."
Bonhoeffer's own great personal sacrifice and suffering in World
War II was never leavened by that anguish of "defeat" which came
to both victors and vanquished in the outcome of the war—the
sense of a profound frustration of corporate historical purpose.

Thus, it is not surprising that Bonhoeffer's understanding of existentialism is superficial. And, I think, it was not by chance that his later thought subsequently inspired a "new theology" and found its appeal chiefly among theologians of the "postwar generation," those anxious to leave behind the heavy hand of history. Also it is not surprising that in the hands of this new generation of theologians Bonhoeffer's theology has "moved off" in so many different directions and yet sustained so few theological results.

"Between the times" we can expect and bear, as it were, a measure of theological frolic. But "between the times" the past becomes very distant and the future too near for theology to be trenchantly framed. We do not say here that history provides the content of theology but only that the times of testing—of a culture and a tradition—demand a sober weighing. Of this we can be sure: the gospel knows a winnowing of history and yet, beyond that, it points to a "dancing before the Lord" that catches up not the young alone, but the weary and the aged as well.

Notes

The following abbreviations are used in the notes:

CD	Bonhoeffer, *The Cost of Discipleship*
DB	Bethge, *Dietrich Bonhoeffer: Theologe, Christ, Zeitgenosse*
DB (E.T.)	Bethge, *Dietrich Bonhoeffer: Man of Vision, Man of Courage*
DTDB	Feil, *Die Theologie Dietrich Bonhoeffers*
DBTR	Dumas, *Dietrich Bonhoeffer, Theologian of Reality*
GS	Bonhoeffer, *Gesammelte Schriften* (4 vols.)
LPP	Bonhoeffer, *Letters and Papers from Prison* (enlarged ed.)
NRS	Bonhoeffer, *No Rusty Swords*
TSTB	Moltmann and Weissbach, *Two Studies in the Theology of Bonhoeffer*

CHAPTER 1. THE IMPACT OF
BONHOEFFER'S LIFE AND THOUGHT

1. Eberhard Bethge, "The Challenge of Dietrich Bonhoeffer's Life and Theology," *The Chicago Theological Seminary Register,* Vol. LI, No. 2 (Feb. 1961), p. 2.

2. *Ibid.,* pp. 2–3.

3. Eberhard Bethge, *Dietrich Bonhoeffer: Theologe, Christ, Zeitgenosse* (Munich: Chr. Kaiser Verlag, 1967), pp. 998–999 (my translation). Cf. the

English translation, *Dietrich Bonhoeffer: Man of Vision, Man of Courage,* tr. by Eric Mosbacher *et al.* (Harper & Row, Publishers, Inc., 1970), p. 794. Hereafter the German title will be abbreviated as *DB* and the English translation as *DB* (E.T.).

4. Jürgen Moltmann, *Herrschaft Christi und soziale Wirklichkeit nach Dietrich Bonhoeffer* (Munich: Chr. Kaiser Verlag, 1959); an English translation, "The Lordship of Christ and Human Society," appears in Jürgen Moltmann and Jürgen Weissbach, *Two Studies in the Theology of Bonhoeffer,* tr. by Reginald H. Fuller and Ilse Fuller (Charles Scribner's Sons, 1967). Moltmann's study is hereafter referred to as Moltmann, *TSTB.* Also in this connection see Gerhard Ebeling's 1955 study, "Die 'nicht-religiöse Interpretation biblischer Begriffe,' " published in *Die mündige Welt,* Vol. II (Munich: Chr. Kaiser Verlag, 1956).

5. John D. Godsey, *The Theology of Dietrich Bonhoeffer* (The Westminster Press, 1960); Hanfried Müller, *Von der Kirche zur Welt* (Leipzig: Koehler und Amelang, 1961). Quotations from Müller's book are my translation.

6. John A. T. Robinson, *Honest to God* (The Westminster Press, 1963).

7. Cf. Bethge's very similar assessment of these developments, *DB* (E.T.), p. 794. See also Reginald Fuller's introduction to Moltmann, *TSTB,* pp. 12–13.

8. Paul M. van Buren, *The Secular Meaning of the Gospel: Based on an Analysis of Its Language* (The Macmillan Company, 1963).

9. Paul M. van Buren, "Bonhoeffer's Paradox: Living with God without God," *Union Seminary Quarterly Review,* Vol. XXIII, No. 1 (Fall 1967), pp. 45–47.

10. Harvey Cox, *The Secular City* (The Macmillan Company, 1965).

11. See Cox's discussion of Tillich and Barth in *ibid.,* pp. 81–84; cf. pp. 240–241. Regarding Bonhoeffer's influence on Cox, cf. Daniel Callahan (ed.), *The Secular City Debate* (The Macmillan Company, 1966), p. 1.

12. For Cox, the rejection of "religion" and "metaphysics" not only meant a call to reappraise the traditional conception of God (see Cox, *The Secular City,* pp. 260–268) but also entailed a peremptory dismissal of the important existentialist tradition (see *ibid.,* pp. 67–68, 80–81, 251–253). In *The Secular City* one can observe that Cox seems not to have gone very far beyond the attitudes toward existentialism expressed by Bonhoeffer in *Letters and Papers from Prison;* see enlarged edition of the latter, ed. by Eberhard Bethge (The Macmillan Company, 1972), pp. 326–327, 344–346. (Hereafter this title will be abbreviated as *LPP.*)

13. Harvey Cox, "Beyond Bonhoeffer?" *Commonweal,* Vol. LXXXII, No. 21 (Sept. 17, 1965), p. 654.

14. Thomas J. J. Altizer and William Hamilton, *Radical Theology and the Death of God* (The Bobbs-Merrill Company, Inc., 1966), p. 36.

15. *The Minneapolis Star,* Dec. 17, 1966, p. 10A. The reference is to a statement in Bonhoeffer's letter of July 16, 1944: "Before God and with God we live without God" (*LPP,* p. 360).

16. Paul L. Lehmann, "Faith and Worldliness in Bonhoeffer's Thought," *Union Seminary Quarterly Review,* Vol. XXIII, No. 1 (Fall 1967), p. 34; see also pp. 41–44. For something of Hamilton's attitude toward these criticisms, see his review of Bethge's biography of Bonhoeffer in *Journal of the American Academy of Religion,* Vol. XXXIX, No. 3 (Sept. 1971), pp. 360–362.

17. Jaroslav Pelikan, "He Inspired the Death of God," *Saturday Review of Literature,* Vol. L, No. 11 (March 18, 1967), p. 30.

18. *LPP,* p. 360.

19. Cf. Milan Machoveč, *Marxismus und dialektische Theologie* (Zurich: Evangelische Verlag, 1965). Bonhoeffer's strong rejection of Christian "otherworldliness" and "religion" certainly contributed to the dialogue.

20. Such is the view of Eberhard Bethge (personal interview, June 1970). I am inclined to see a more direct influence of Bonhoeffer upon Moltmann, especially in Bonhoeffer's concept of the relation of the "ultimate" to the "penultimate" as set forth in his *Ethics,* ed. by Eberhard Bethge, tr. by Neville Horton Smith (The Macmillan Company, 1965), pp. 120–187.

21. Roger Shinn, "Political Theology in the Crossfire," *Perspective,* Vol. XIII, No. 1 (Winter 1972), pp. 59–79.

22. *Ibid.,* p. 62.

23. *Ibid.*

24. Cf. report on the Wayne State University conference on the German church struggle, *The Detroit News,* March 21, 1970, p. 6A.

25. Some of this analysis is applicable also to groups of Christians in the "Third World" who struggle against reactionary political and social systems.

26. William Kuhns, *In Pursuit of Dietrich Bonhoeffer* (Doubleday & Company, Inc., Image Books, 1969), pp. 281–282.

27. John A. Phillips, *Christ for Us in the Theology of Dietrich Bonhoeffer* (Harper & Row, Publishers, Inc., 1967), p. 245. Phillips' study was first

published in England under the title *The Form of Christ in the World* (London: William Collins Sons & Co., Ltd., 1967).

28. Heinrich Ott, *Reality and Faith: The Theological Legacy of Dietrich Bonhoeffer* (Fortress Press, 1972), p. 32.

2. THE QUESTIONS OF STATURE AND CONTINUITY OF THOUGHT

1. The latter presupposes that theology in the Christian tradition is finally inseparable from the life of the church.

2. Another factor that also seems to have played a role is the increasing accessibility of the Bonhoeffer source materials that came about during the middle and late 1950's. Bonhoeffer thereby became an occasion of research. The mass of materials demanded assimilation, and in this situation the unifying hypothesis rather naturally commanded the greatest attention.

3. These phrases were titles of popular theological series published during the 1960's: *New Frontiers in Theology; New Theology* (No. 1, etc.).

4. Eckhard Minthe, "Bonhoeffer's Influence in Germany," *Andover Newton Quarterly,* n.s., Vol. II, No. 1 (Sept. 1961), pp. 15–16.

5. Quoted in Phillips, *Christ for Us . . . ,* p. 251. (Cf. *Die mündige Welt: Dem Andenken Dietrich Bonhoeffers* (Munich: Chr. Kaiser Verlag, 1955), p. 121. It should be noted that Barth, in 1967, essentially reiterated this assessment of Bonhoeffer in his letter to Bethge following publication of the latter's biography of Bonhoeffer. See Karl Barth, *Fragments Grave and Gay* (London: Wm. Collins Sons & Co., Ltd., 1971), pp. 119–122.

6. Phillips, *Christ for Us . . . ,* p. 251 (translation revised somewhat). Cf. also Karl Barth, *Church Dogmatics,* Vol. III/2 (Edinburgh: T. & T. Clark, 1958), pp. 194–195; Vol. III/4 (1961), pp. 4, 21–22; Vol. IV/2 (1958), pp. 533–534, 641.

7. Cf. Phillips, *Christ for Us . . . ,* pp. 28–36, 245; Bethge, *DB* (E.T.), pp. 138–140; Benjamin A. Reist, *The Promise of Bonhoeffer* (J. B. Lippincott Company, 1969), p. 38.

8. Gerhard Ebeling, *Word and Faith,* tr. by James W. Leitch (Fortress Press, 1963), pp. 103–126, especially p. 105. Cf. also *Die mündige Welt,* Vol. II, pp. 12–73. Ebeling's analysis was presented as a paper to one of the conferences of "friends and pupils of Bonhoeffer" that were held periodically beginning in 1954. Some of the proceedings of these conferences were subsequently published at intervals in several volumes under

the title *Die mündige Welt.* This series of conferences, terminating in the year 1962, had much to do with establishing the new estimate of Bonhoeffer's stature, despite occasional dissenting opinions expressed in these meetings.

9. See above, note 4 of Chapter 1.

10. Moltmann, *TSTB,* p. 56. Moltmann's argument here will be explored more fully below, in Chapter 3.

11. This is a translation of the German title of Bethge's book; see above, note 3 of Chapter 1.

12. Müller, *Von der Kirche zur Welt.* The book has not been translated into English, but the gist of Müller's interpretation is available in Ronald Gregor Smith (ed.), *World Come of Age* (Fortress Press, 1967), pp. 182–214. Müller completed his study of Bonhoeffer in 1956 as a doctoral dissertation and did not have access to all of the research materials that became available later, though he points out that Bethge made much unpublished material available to him.

13. Müller, *Von der Kirche zur Welt,* pp. 5–6, 147–156. Cf. Smith (ed.), *World Come of Age,* pp. 202–208.

14. Müller, *Von der Kirche zur Welt,* pp. 9–10.

15. Godsey, *The Theology of Dietrich Bonhoeffer.* Godsey's work was originally submitted as a doctoral dissertation to the Theological Faculty of the University of Basel in 1958. His interpretation is not indebted to either Moltmann or Müller.

16. *Ibid.,* p. 264.

17. *Ibid.,* p. 266. Italics Godsey's.

18. *Ibid.,* p. 271; cf. also p. 17. Müller essentially argues for the abandonment of ecclesiology by the later Bonhoeffer. See below, Chapter 3.

19. Phillips, *Christ for Us . . . ,* pp. 27–28.

20. *Ibid.,* p. 83.

21. The "German Christians" were a faction within the German Evangelical Church. They were strongly supportive of National Socialism and sought to enlist the church in its cause.

22. Phillips, *Christ for Us . . . ,* p. 103.

23. *Ibid.,* p. 104.

24. *Ibid.*

25. *Ibid.,* p. 27.

26. *Ibid.* To be fair to Godsey at this point, I do not think that Godsey in fact argues that Bonhoeffer's concern was "primarily" ecclesiological.

27. Heinrich Ott, *Reality and Faith,* pp. 65–66. Ott mentions Barth's

assessment of Bonhoeffer, attempts to assimilate it and still argue for continuity (cf. pp. 67–68). It is unfortunate that Ott omitted from his quotation of Barth's 1952 letter to Landessuperintendent Herrenbruck the specifics of Barth's complaint, which then would have demanded discussion by Ott (see Phillips, *Christ for Us . . .* , pp. 250–253). One should also note that Ott's "dialogical" methodology (Ott, *Reality and Faith,* pp. 69–93) is so imprecise that a delineation of important problems and incongruities in Bonhoeffer's thought is hardly to be expected.

28. Ott, *Reality and Faith,* pp. 370–373, 392, 393. "This view of Christ as the truly real upholding all reality is maintained throughout his work, it may be with varying nuances, but without any material break" (p. 168).

29. *Ibid.,* pp. 168–170.

30. *Ibid.,* p. 63.

31. *Ibid.,* p. 62.

32. This is not to say, however, that Ott, Moltmann, Godsey, and Bethge are all agreed on the nature of Bonhoeffer's ecclesiology.

33. *Ibid.,* p. 19.

34. *Ibid.,* p. 20.

35. *Ibid.,* p. 167. Italics Ott's.

36. Eberhard Bethge, book review, *Union Seminary Quarterly Review,* Vol. XXIII, No. 1 (Fall 1967), p. 95.

37. *Ibid.*

38. André Dumas, *Une Theologie de la réalité: Dietrich Bonhoeffer* (Geneva: Editions Labor et Fides, S.A., 1968). English translation: *Dietrich Bonhoeffer: Theologian of Reality,* tr. by Robert McAfee Brown (The Macmillan Company, 1971). Quotations will be from the latter, referred to hereafter as *DBTR.*

39. Dumas, *DBTR,* p. 30.

40. *Ibid.,* pp. 30–31.

41. *Ibid.,* p. 31; cf. also p. 217. For an assessment of Dumas's "Hegelian" interpretation, see below, Chapter 3, especially notes 99 and 101.

42. Dumas, *DBTR,* pp. 217, 234–235, 294–295.

43. *Ibid.,* p. 235.

44. E.g., James W. Woelfel, *Bonhoeffer's Theology: Classical and Revolutionary* (Abingdon Press, 1970); and Reist, *The Promise of Bonhoeffer.*

45. Ernst Feil, *Die Theologie Dietrich Bonhoeffers* (Munich: Chr. Kaiser Verlag, 1971). Hereafter this work is referred to as *DTDB.* Translations from it are mine.

46. *Ibid.,* pp. 322–323. Cf. Paul Lehmann's earlier statement of a very similar point of view: "Faith and Worldliness in Bonhoeffer's Thought," *Union Seminary Quarterly Review,* Vol. XXIII, No. 1 (Fall 1967).

47. Feil, *DTDB,* pp. 55–56, 61–62, 127–133.

48. *Ibid.,* pp. 71–72. Reist's interpretation of Bonhoeffer's thought, following Lehmann, is similar to this. See Reist, *The Promise of Bonhoeffer.*

49. Feil, *DTDB,* pp. 275–285.

50. *Ibid.,* p. 180.

51. *Ibid.,* pp. 23–26, 288–289.

52. *Ibid.,* pp. 320–323.

53. *Ibid.,* p. 290.

3. INTERPRETATIVE POINTS OF DIFFERENCE

1. Dietrich Bonhoeffer, *Gesammelte Schriften,* 4 vols. (Munich: Chr. Kaiser Verlag, 1958–1961). Hereafter these volumes of "collected writings" will be referred to as *GS* I, etc. Unless otherwise indicated, translations from this source are mine.

2. Ebeling, *Word and Faith,* p. 103.

3. *Ibid.,* p. 105.

4. *Ibid.*

5. *Ibid.,* p. 104. What is only tentatively discussed here is later presupposed. Cf. *ibid.,* p. 142n1, especially p. 156n6.

6. Ott, *Reality and Faith,* pp. 116–120. Cf. also Moltmann, *TSTB,* p. 66.

7. Ott, *Reality and Faith,* p. 107. Cf. also p. 171; pp. 371–372 offer further argument.

8. Müller, *Von der Kirche zur Welt,* pp. 9, 31–33.

9. *Ibid.,* pp. 354–356; see also pp. 42–51. The issue that Müller here raises, especially in regard to the systematic coherence of Bonhoeffer's *Ethics,* deserves wider discussion than it has been given. Cf. Rainer Mayer, *Christuswirklichkeit* (Stuttgart: Calwer Verlag, 1969), pp. 168–169, 294n30. Quotations from Mayer are my translation.

10. Mayer, *Christuswirklichkeit,* p. 227; cf. also pp. 219–227.

11. Moltmann, *TSTB,* pp. 21–22, 56.

12. *Ibid.,* p. 56. Here we have an assertion similar to Mayer's noting of a shift, but again, not a breach, between *Ethics* and *Letters and Papers from Prison;* cf. Mayer, *Christuswirklichkeit,* p. 225.

13. *Creation and Fall* was first published in 1937: *Schöpfung und Fall* (Munich: Chr. Kaiser Verlag). It represents lectures delivered by Bonhoeffer at the University of Berlin during the winter semester of 1932–1933.

14. Moltmann indicates some awareness of problems at this point. Cf. Moltmann, *TSTB*, p. 71.

15. Ott, *Reality and Faith*, pp. 66–67.

16. *Ibid.*, p. 66.

17. Ott, in fact, virtually rules out the possibility of contradiction; cf. *ibid.*, p. 82.

18. *Ibid.*, pp. 74–95.

19. *Ibid.*, p. 70.

20. *Ibid.*, p. 89.

21. *Ibid.*, p. 91.

22. *Ibid.*, p. 92.

23. Eberhard Bethge, book review, *Union Seminary Quarterly Review*, Vol. XXIII, No. 1 (Fall 1967), p. 95.

24. Mayer, *Christuswirklichkeit*, p. 33.

25. See especially, Dumas, *DBTR*, pp. 269–280.

26. *Ibid.*, pp. 30–37, 78–83, 190–196, 216–217, 232–235, 278, 294–295.

27. See below, Chapter 5.

28. Dumas, *DBTR*, p. 37; cf. also p. 154.

29. *Ibid.*, pp. 31–35, 287–292.

30. Woelfel, *Bonhoeffer's Theology: Classical and Revolutionary,* also belongs in this grouping.

31. Dumas's analysis is something of an exception to this statement. Dumas *does* attempt to deal with these matters, but whether he is able to accord them adequate weight is debatable. In my opinion Dumas's forced Hegelian analysis inhibits this effort and in the end cancels out a contradictory but more valid interpretation of Bonhoeffer that Dumas himself proposes; cf. *DBTR*, pp. 137–138, 167–168. These latter two passages should be compared with his statement of the Hegelian hypothesis (see above, note 26 of this chapter). The two patterns of assessment can be reconciled only by means of an "existentialized" Hegelianism (cf. *DBTR*, pp. 219n7, 233n32) that apparently can even claim Kierkegaard as a friend (cf. *DBTR*, pp. 118–138).

32. Paul Lehmann, book review, *Union Seminary Quarterly Review*, Vol. XXIII, No. 1 (Fall 1967), pp. 99–100. It is not likely that Lehmann here intends also the elimination of a scholarly probing of Bonhoeffer's

unreliability and/or "impulsiveness" as a subject of theological concern.

33. *Ibid.,* p. 104.

34. Moltmann, *TSTB,* p. 56. This statement of Moltmann is very close to Dumas's assertion, just quoted, that a man's life will put his thought to the test, rather than create it.

35. Lehmann, despite the previously cited exchange with Bethge, really is sympathetic with this latter approach; cf. Lehmann, "Faith and Worldliness . . . ," *loc. cit.,* p. 36.

36. Müller, *Von der Kirche zur Welt,* p. 35.

37. *Ibid.,* pp. 34 ff.

38. *Ibid.,* pp. 37–40.

39. *Ibid.,* pp. 42–47.

40. *Ibid.,* pp. 47–51. It is interesting to note the tendency in Müller to point up incongruities and inadequacies in Bonhoeffer's theology, sustained as Müller himself seems to be by the Marxist thesis of a logic and coherence to the course of events (historical determinism).

41. Phillips, *Christ for Us . . . ,* p. 23. In describing Müller's interpretation of Bonhoeffer as a "theology of reaction," Phillips means to deny that Bonhoeffer was simply responding to political circumstance.

42. *Ibid.,* p. 28.

43. *Ibid.,* pp. 74–75.

44. *Ibid.,* pp. 128–131.

45. Woelfel's work, *Bonhoeffer's Theology: Classical and Revolutionary* should also be mentioned as an exception. Although Woelfel describes his 1970 book as a "considerably revised version" of a 1966 doctoral dissertation, the revision does not make use of Bethge's 1967 biography.

46. Mayer, *Christuswirklichkeit,* p. 42.

47. *Ibid.,* pp. 223–225. Mayer also suggests that internal systematic difficulties had a part to play in this collapse (cf. pp. 219–221).

48. *Ibid.,* pp. 23–31.

49. *Ibid.,* p. 225; but cf. also p. 221, where Mayer suggests that only "a little push" was needed to bring the system down.

50. Feil, *DTDB,* pp. 171, 198.

51. Ernst Feil, book review, *Evangelische Kommentaren,* Vol. III, No. 3 (March 1970), pp. 176–177.

52. Feil, *DTDB,* pp. 81–85, especially p. 85; cf. also pp. 62–64.

53. *Ibid.,* pp. 28–29.

54. *Ibid.,* pp. 122–126. Reist's interpretation, set forth earlier than Feil's, very much parallels this argument.

55. Feil, *DTDB*, pp. 77–80. Cf. Eberhard Bethge, "Turning Points in Bonhoeffer's Life and Thought," *Union Seminary Quarterly Review*, Vol. XXIII, No. 1 (Fall 1967), pp. 7–8; *DB* (E.T.), pp. 153–156.

56. Müller, *Von der Kirche zur Welt*, pp. 264–265.

57. *Ibid.*, pp. 251–252.

58. *Ibid.*, p. 406.

59. *Ibid.*, pp. 354–356.

60. *Ibid.*, pp. 258–259, 394–398, especially 398, 418–442. Cf. H. Müller in *Die mündige Welt*, Vol. IV (Munich: Chr. Kaiser Verlag, 1963), pp. 69–71. Cf. also R. Gregor Smith (ed.), *World Come of Age*, pp. 202–205. For criticism of Müller's views on the church, see *Die mündige Welt*, Vol. IV, pp. 169–174; Feil, *DTDB*, 392–396; Dumas, *DBTR*, pp. 252–253; Mayer, *Christuswirklichkeit*, pp. 154–156. The ecclesiological theme will be discussed further below, in Chapter 4.

61. Phillips, *Christ for Us . . .* , pp. 24–25.

62. *Ibid.*, p. 25.

63. *LPP*, p. 317.

64. *Ibid.*, p. 329.

65. Phillips, *Christ for Us . . .* , p. 25.

66. *Ibid.*, p. 26.

67. Cf. *ibid.*, pp. 230–231.

68. Mayer, *Christuswirklichkeit*, p. 226. But Mayer also holds that something more can be said about the new form of the church in Bonhoeffer's later thought than Phillips allows; cf. pp. 271–280.

69. Godsey asserts that "Christology includes ecclesiology within itself"; see Godsey, *The Theology of Dietrich Bonhoeffer*, p. 264.

70. The one exception to this description is Feil, who does not regard Bonhoeffer's earliest work as essentially Christological in orientation.

71. Moltmann, *TSTB*, p. 42.

72. *Ibid.*, p. 43.

73. Dietrich Bonhoeffer, *The Communion of Saints: A Dogmatic Inquiry into the Sociology of the Church*, tr. by R. Gregor Smith (Harper & Row, Publishers, Inc., 1963), pp. 113–114. (Note: This passage is not quoted by Moltmann in its entirety; see Moltmann *TSTB*, p. 44.)

74. Moltmann, *TSTB*, p. 44.

75. Bonhoeffer, *Ethics*, pp. 224–262.

76. Moltmann, *TSTB*, p. 56. John Godsey's interpretation of Bonhoeffer's Christology is fairly similar to Moltmann's at this point. Godsey accents Bonhoeffer's growing awareness of the scope of Christ's lordship,

though he does not stress "vicarious representation" and "deputyship" in the manner of Moltmann; cf. Godsey, *The Theology of Dietrich Bonhoeffer*, pp. 264–272.

77. Moltmann, *TSTB*, p. 64.

78. *LPP*, pp. 360–361.

79. Müller, *Von der Kirche zur Welt*, pp. 355, 386–387.

80. *Ibid.*, p. 389.

81. *Ibid.*, p. 390.

82. *Ibid.*

83. Phillips, *Christ for Us* . . . , pp. 69–70.

84. *Ibid.*, pp. 80–83.

85. *Ibid.*, pp. 126–127.

86. *Ibid.*, p. 83.

87. *Ibid.*, p. 104. But cf. also *ibid.*, pp. 224–225, where some of the clear-cut distinctions that Phillips establishes in the first half of his study become somewhat less clear.

88. Bonhoeffer, *LPP*, p. 275.

89. Ott, *Reality and Faith*, p. 370.

90. *Ibid.*, p. 168.

91. *Ibid.*

92. *Ibid.*, p. 171.

93. *Ibid.*, p. 167.

94. *Ibid.*, pp. 188.

95. *Ibid.*, p. 176; cf. also p. 366.

96. Dumas, *DBTR*, p. 276.

97. *Ibid.*, pp. 215–235.

98. *Ibid.*, p. 217. Dumas's assertion is exaggerated; for example, nowhere in the 1933 Christology lectures does the term *Stellvertretung* appear.

99. *Ibid.* It is difficult to reconcile this statement and the whole of Dumas's Hegelian interpretation with a statement such as the following, made by Bonhoeffer in 1931 in an article he wrote in English, entitled "Concerning the Christian Idea of God": "No man can reveal God because God is absolutely free personality. Every human attempt to discover God, to unveil his secret reality, is hopeless because of God's being personality. All such attempts remain in the sphere of the idea. Personality as reality is beyond idea. So that even the self-revelation of personality cannot be executed in the sphere of idea. The idea is in the sphere of generality. Personality exists in 'onceness' because of its freedom. The only place

where 'onceness' might occur is history. Therefore, revelation of personality—that is to say, the self-revelation of God—must take place in history, if at all." (*GS* III, p. 104.) Cf. also, Mayer, *Christuswirklichkeit,* pp. 96–97.

100. Dumas, *DBTR,* p. 216.

101. *Ibid.* It should be pointed out that Dumas provides a second level of Christological interpretation in connection with an earlier discussion of *Letters and Papers from Prison;* cf. *DBTR,* pp. 190–193. This second level of interpretation is substantively more "Hegelian" (though referring to Bonhoeffer's later thought) than is Dumas's primary Christological analysis (which is based on Bonhoeffer's earlier thought). This pattern runs counter to Dumas's assertion: "Hegel gave Bonhoeffer his basic stimulus when he was a student . . . and when he was a young professor, after which he went on to work out his own point of view" (Dumas, *DBTR,* p. 217). It should be stated that Dumas is not uncritical of *some* of the "Hegelian" tendencies in Bonhoeffer's thought; cf. *ibid.,* pp. 193–197, 217, 232–235.

102. See above, p. 42.

103. Mayer, *Christuswirklichkeit,* pp. 219–221.

104. *Ibid.,* pp. 92–93.

105. *Ibid.*

106. *Ibid.,* p. 41.

107. *Ibid.,* pp. 73–77.

108. *Ibid.,* p. 60.

109. *Ibid.,* pp. 60–61; cf. also pp. 92–96.

110. See above, p. 29.

111. Mayer, *Christuswirklichkeit,* p. 197n165.

112. Mayer's exposition of Bonhoeffer's Christology and its relation to the development of Bonhoeffer's theology is a very complex one which identifies certain inner tensions, incomplete formulations, and historical experiences as playing roles in the development of his ontology. (Cf. *ibid.,* pp. 40–42, 84–90, 92–96, 103–112, 164–167, 219–227, 287–291.)

113. Feil, *DTDB,* p. 171n57. The reference is to *The Cost of Discipleship* (The Macmillan Company, 1963), p. 255n1. Hereafter this work is abbreviated as *CD.*

114. Feil, *DTDB,* p. 198n35.

115. See the discussion of Feil's methodology earlier in this chapter.

116. Feil, *DTDB,* pp. 142–149.

117. *Ibid.,* pp. 147–148.

118. *Ibid.,* pp. 149–156, especially pp. 149, 156.

119. In connection with the use of the term "mediator" Feil notes the

possible influence upon Bonhoeffer of Emil Brunner's 1926 Christological study, *The Mediator;* see Feil, *DTDB,* pp. 217–218.

120. Feil, *DTDB,* pp. 175–176.

121. *Ibid.,* pp. 177–181, especially p. 181.

122. *Ibid.,* pp. 178–179, especially n. 12; p. 192n12; and p. 215.

123. *Ibid.,* pp. 181–184.

124. *Ibid.,* pp. 189–191, 197–198. Cf. also Reist, *The Promise of Bonhoeffer,* pp. 77–79.

125. Feil, *DTDB,* p. 203.

126. *Ibid.,* p. 209.

127. *Ibid.,* p. 219.

128. *Ibid.,* p. 209.

129. *Ibid.,* p. 210.

130. Bonhoeffer, *Act and Being,* tr. by Bernard Noble (Harper & Row, Publishers, Inc., 1961), pp. 90–91.

131. Bonhoeffer, *GS* I, p. 61.

132. Bethge, "The Challenge of Dietrich Bonhoeffer's Life and Theology," *loc. cit.,* p. 8.

133. *Ibid.*

134. *Ibid.,* p. 9. On Christological differences between Bonhoeffer and Barth, with further references, see Feil, *DTDB,* pp. 215–216, nn. 4, 5, 6.

135. Bethge, "The Challenge of Dietrich Bonhoeffer's Life and Theology," *loc. cit.,* p. 11.

136. *Ibid.,* p. 12.

137. *Ibid.,* p. 13.

138. Eberhard Bethge, book review, *Union Seminary Quarterly Review,* Vol. XXIII, No. 1 (Fall 1967), p. 95.

139. *Ibid.,* p. 96.

140. Ott, *Reality and Faith,* p. 158n23; cf. also p. 138n12, pp. 190, 266–268, 366.

141. *Ibid.,* pp. 392–393; cf. also pp. 429–431, 449–451.

142. *Ibid.,* p. 236n26; cf. also pp. 192–195.

143. See *Ethics,* pp. 88–109; *LPP,* pp. 279–281, 294–300, 325–329, 359–361.

144. Ott, *Reality and Faith,* p. 107; cf. also pp. 45–46n9.

145. Dumas, *DBTR,* pp. 30–31; see the quotation from Bonhoeffer in note 99 of this chapter.

146. Dumas, *DBTR,* p. 231.

147. *Ibid.,* p. 230.

148. *Ibid.* One might observe that in his statement of Bonhoeffer's view of reality Mayer's ontological position is at variance with the positions of both Ott and Dumas. For Mayer, "reality" was "the act-being unity" of Christ, which for a time was projected as a means of structuring all reality.

149. Feil, *DTDB,* pp. 223–224, 367–368, 386–387. Feil asserts: "The continuity of the engagement of the disciple is the presupposition from which Bonhoeffer developed *(a posteriori)* his theology" (p. 130).

150. *Ibid.,* pp. 290–292; cf. pp. 189–191.

151. *Ibid.,* pp. 317–323, especially p. 323.

152. *Ibid.,* pp. 355–368.

153. *Ibid.,* p. 369.

154. *Ibid.,* p. 368.

155. *Ibid.,* p. 370.

4. ASSESSMENT OF POINTS AT ISSUE

1. To cite a case in point, Moltmann, in his early study of Bonhoeffer, attempts to equate the idea of deputyship as found in *Ethics* with that of vicarious representation as treated in *The Communion of Saints.* He does this despite the fact that he himself identifies a cosmocratic motif in the *Ethics* that is hardly to be equated with the context of Bonhoeffer's statement of substitutionary atonement found in *The Communion of Saints.* Dorothee Sölle may be wrong in aspects of her overall argument, but her understanding of the import of Bonhoeffer's later statement of deputyship has much to be said for it; cf. Dorothee Sölle, *Christ the Representative: An Essay in Theology After the Death of God,* tr. by David Lewis (Fortress Press, 1967), pp. 93–97, especially pp. 96–97.

2. Cf. Feil, *DTDB,* pp. 127–129.

3. *Ibid.,* p. 128n6. Feil lists the many scholars besides himself who follow this tack.

4. *LPP,* pp. 275–276. The passage has been quoted at length because there are nuances of meaning that are often lost by abridgment. Feil quotes the passage only in part; cf. Feil, *DTDB,* p. 129.

5. Feil, *DTDB,* pp. 131–132; quoted here from *LPP,* p. 219. This passage is also quoted frequently by other interpreters in support of the argument for an underlying unity to Bonhoeffer's life and thought.

6. *GS* I, p. 26; cf. the English translation of abridged *GS:* Dietrich Bonhoeffer, *No Rusty Swords* (Letters, Lectures and Notes from His Collected Works, Vol. I, 1928–1935), ed. by Edwin H. Robertson and John

Bowden (Harper & Row, Publishers, Inc., 1965), p. 149. This title is hereafter abbreviated as *NRS.*

7. *LPP,* p. 369.

8. *Ibid.,* p. 279.

9. *Ibid.,* pp. 299–300. A portion of this latter quotation is cited and discussed by Feil, *DTDB,* pp. 130–131.

10. Feil, *DTDB,* p. 132.

11. Still another illustration of this phenomenon—but more question-able, I think, than other interpretations—is the recently published article by William J. Peck, "From Cain to the Death Camps: An Essay on Bonhoeffer and Judaism," *Union Seminary Quarterly Review,* Vol. XXVIII, No. 2 (Winter 1973), pp. 158–176. Peck's argument in support of an increasingly formative role for Bonhoeffer's opposition to anti-Semitism and the effort to relate this feature of Bonhoeffer's life to the later conceptualization of "religion" and the "world come of age" (secularism) fails to note Feil's important research on the role of Dilthey in all of this. Peck's neglect of the secondary source material seems almost studied and deprives him, it would seem, of helpful insight.

12. Feil, *DTDB,* pp. 55–57.

13. *Ibid.,* pp. 72–80.

14. *Ibid.,* p. 131. And at another point Feil asserts: " 'Coming-of-age' *(Mündigkeit)* is here primarily *not* a category of individual maturation but a category of epochal, social emancipation" (*ibid.,* p. 370).

15. Godsey, *The Theology of Dietrich Bonhoeffer,* pp. 17, 264.

16. See Feil, *DTDB,* pp. 142–149.

17. *Ibid.,* pp. 392–396.

18. *Ibid.,* p. 371.

19. *Ibid.,* p. 394.

20. *Ibid.*

21. *Ibid.,* pp. 395–396.

22. Cf. Bonhoeffer, *The Communion of Saints,* pp. 36–37, 118–136.

23. Feil notes the conclusions of German scholarship in this matter; cf. Feil, *DTDB,* pp. 30n7, 33n19. Cf. also Bethge, *DB* (E.T.), p. 59.

24. Cf. Bethge, *DB* (E.T.), pp. 231–239.

25. The work of Kierkegaard that is chiefly cited by Bonhoeffer is *Fear and Trembling.* He refers also to an article about Kierkegaard by Heinrich Barth. Cf. Bonhoeffer, *The Communion of Saints,* pp. 211, 224–225, 242.

26. Bonhoeffer, *The Communion of Saints,* p. 212. The thought of Bonhoeffer at this point is very dubious. In the light of *Fear and Trembling*

it is difficult to see how Bonhoeffer can say that Kierkegaard's "ethical person exists only in the concrete situation, but it has no necessary connection with a concrete Thou. The I itself establishes the Thou; it is not established by it." (*The Communion of Saints,* p. 212.)

27. Woelfel, *Bonhoeffer's Theology: Classical and Revolutionary,* pp. 84–88. Woelfel states that one can speak here only of "parallels" between Kierkegaard and Bonhoeffer, maintaining that "of Kierkegaard's explicit influence on Bonhoeffer we have very little knowledge . . . ," and that "beyond brief and occasional references . . . we have nothing to go on" (p. 313n38).

28. Dumas, *DBTR,* pp. 118–129.

29. Bethge calls attention to Vogel's work in the third German edition of his Bonhoeffer biography (referred to by Feil, *DTDB,* p. 277n39).

30. Feil, *DTDB,* p. 277n39.

31. Dumas, *DBTR,* p. 132.

32. *Ibid.*

33. E.g., Dietrich Bonhoeffer, *Life Together,* tr. by John W. Doberstein (Harper & Row, Publishers, Inc., 1954), pp. 24–26.

34. *Ibid.,* p. 60.

35. *LPP,* pp. 280–281, 300, 317, 329. Cf. Phillips, *Christ for Us . . . ,* pp. 24–25.

36. *NRS,* pp. 65–69, especially pp. 68–69 (*GS* III, pp. 80–84). Cf. also *Act and Being,* pp. 12–13, 102–103.

37. *LPP,* pp. 373, 382. A passage from *Act and Being,* pp. 182–183, seems to come close to the thought of the prison letter of July 27, 1944; but in the latter it takes on new meaning in the light of a revised world view (Dilthey); that is to say, Bonhoeffer seems on the point of de-eschatologizing the old Lutheran baptismal formulation. He no longer suggests that it is "the wishful regret of theology, when it must speak of faith and unbelief, of election and rejection." In this same connection one should point out that Bonhoeffer's later interpretation of confessionalism (*LPP,* p. 382) contrasts sharply with his earlier view. Cf. Dietrich Bonhoeffer, *Christ the Center,* tr. by John Bowden (Harper & Row, Publishers, Inc., 1966), p. 78: "But there can be no confession without saying 'In the light of Christ, this is true and this is false.' The concept of heresy belongs necessarily and irrevocably with that of confession."

38. Feil, *DTDB,* pp. 149–150. This judgment of Feil must be qualified somewhat in the light of Bonhoeffer's later interest in an "unconscious

Christianity" and his attack on Barth's "positivism of revelation."

39. See above, pp. 50, 61.

40. See above, p. 61.

41. See above, pp. 32–33, 55–56, 58, 61–62.

42. See above, pp. 33, 48, 56, 62.

43. See above, p. 73.

44. *The Communion of Saints,* pp. 25–35.

45. Cf. *ibid.,* pp. 35–37, 49–50.

46. *Ibid.,* pp. 28–35.

47. *Ibid.,* p. 101. Cf. also pp. 89–91, 96–97, 99–101, 104–105.

48. *Ibid.,* pp. 112–114. For Bonhoeffer's distinction between Roman Catholicism and Protestantism at this point, see *ibid.,* pp. 186–187.

49. *Ibid.,* pp. 113–114, 118–135. Cf. Feil, *DTDB,* pp. 146–148.

50. *Act and Being,* pp. 36–48, 118–119.

51. *Ibid.,* pp. 79–89. Cf. Feil, *DTDB,* pp. 149–150, 155–156.

52. *Act and Being,* p. 122; cf. also pp. 91–97, 140–151.

53. Bethge, "The Challenge of Dietrich Bonhoeffer's Life and Theology," *loc. cit.,* p. 10; *DB* (E.T.), p. 164.

54. Bonhoeffer, *Christ the Center,* p. 106.

55. Moltmann's assertion that "deputyship" (i.e., vicarious representation) as a unifying theme of Bonhoeffer's thought is, as already indicated, very dubious. See above, note 1 of this chapter.

56. Martin E. Marty (ed.), *The Place of Bonhoeffer* (Association Press, 1962), pp. 162–164.

57. *The Communion of Saints,* pp. 226–227; *Act and Being,* pp. 90–91, 102–104.

58. *LPP,* p. 369.

59. Bethge, *DB* (E.T.), pp. 153–156.

60. *LPP,* pp. 369–370. Thus there are hints of a "methodism" to be found also in Bonhoeffer's later turn of thought (cf. *LPP,* p. 326).

61. Bethge also argues for the personal basis of *The Cost of Discipleship* —contra Hanfried Müller and also John Phillips, who regard that work as primarily a withdrawal from the world, brought on through the pressure of external events. However, Bethge is more inclined to view this matter of personal quest as an enriching progression rather than as a cause of fluctuating patterns in Bonhoeffer's thought. Cf. Bethge *DB* (E.T.), pp. 158–159, 375–379. Cf. also *CD,* pp. 37–39.

62. See Bonhoeffer's Introduction to *The Cost of Discipleship.* As noted

earlier, Dumas also suggests that with *Life Together* Bonhoeffer was trying to correct an individualistic imbalance in *The Cost of Discipleship* (*DBTR,* p. 132).

63. Admittedly this is a rather subjective judgment, but the varied testimonies of some of those involved in the communal experiment of the pastors' seminary at Finkenwalde tend, I believe, to support this judgment. Cf. Wolf-Dieter Zimmermann and Ronald Gregor Smith (eds.), *I Knew Dietrich Bonhoeffer,* tr. by Käthe Gregor Smith (Harper & Row, Publishers, Inc., 1967), pp. 107–111, 123–137.

64. *CD,* p. 69.

65. *Ibid.*

66. *Ibid.,* pp. 63–64.

67. *Ibid.,* p. 65.

68. *Ibid.,* p. 96.

69. *Ibid.*

70. Cf. *ibid.,* pp. 62, 173, 190–191, 341.

71. *Ibid.,* pp. 263–336.

72. *Ibid.,* p. 339–344.

73. *Ibid.,* p. 59.

74. Cf. Phillips, *Christ for Us . . . ,* pp. 96–102.

75. *CD,* pp. 106–110. This pattern differs, however, from the later *Ethics* as a result of a largely negative definition of "the world"; cf., for example, *CD,* pp. 289–304.

76. *Ibid.,* pp. 62–63.

77. *Ibid.,* pp. 102–103, 307–310.

78. The variety of ways in which Bonhoeffer defines "grace" is also, I think, instructive at this point; cf. *CD,* pp. 41, 47–48, 49, 55, 60, 65, 100–101, 146, 161, 245, 257–258, 273, 298. Lack of clarity is also to be noted on the matter of whether "discipleship" is a call to the many or the few; cf. *ibid.,* pp. 39–41, 58–59, 70, 95–102, 127–128, 141, 211–212, 223–225, 249–253, 272–273, 342.

79. *CD,* p. 289.

80. *Ibid.,* p. 304.

81. The "expanded" view of Christ's lordship is generally recognized by most scholars to be an emerging theme of the *Ethics* (cf. *Ethics,* pp. 68–70, 296–297, 322–323, 361).

82. *Ethics,* pp. 39–40, 51, 188–193.

83. *Ibid.,* pp. 24–26, 242–245, 283.

84. *Ibid.,* pp. 88–109, especially pp. 102–104.

85. *CD*, pp. 162–171.

86. Cf. Bethge, *DB* (E.T.), pp. 428–436.

87. *Ethics*, pp. 55–63.

88. *Ibid.*, p. 55; cf. also pp. 142–143.

89. *Ibid.*, p. 197.

90. Larry L. Rasmussen in *Dietrich Bonhoeffer: Reality and Resistance* (Abingdon Press, 1972) attempts to give a Christological explanation of Bonhoeffer's move away from pacifism (pp. 49–63). Rasmussen's argument is unconvincing. See below, Chapter 5.

91. *Ethics*, p. 225. Again, despite Moltmann's argument, this clearly is not the same idea of vicarious sacrifice that marked *The Communion of Saints*. See above, n.1 of this chapter.

92. *Ibid.*

93. *Ibid.*, p. 224.

94. *Ibid.*, p. 244. The thought here stands in sharp contrast to an important passage in *CD*, pp. 138–139. The critical question to be asked about this particular fragment on "Acceptance of Guilt" and "Conscience" is whether it represents a breakthrough in Christological thought that then leads on to his involvement in the conspiracy, as Rasmussen suggests, or whether it represents ex post facto Christological reflection, following Bonhoeffer's involvement, or anticipated involvement, in conspiracy. Cf. Rasmussen, *Dietrich Bonhoeffer,* especially p. 61n138; see also *Die mündige Welt,* Vol. I, p. 12.

95. *Ethics*, pp. 286, 288–289, 296–299, 320–331.

96. Cf. Bethge, *DB* (E.T.), pp. 377–378.

97. *CD*, pp. 106–110. See above, note 75 of this chapter.

98. *Ethics*, pp. 279–283.

99. *Ibid.*, pp. 64–88.

100. *Ibid.*, pp. 69–72.

101. *Ibid.*, pp. 72–74. Cf. the formal statement: "Jesus is not *a* man. He is *man.*" (P. 72.) More important than this is the description of the actualities of "mankind" that follow.

102. *Ibid.*, pp. 120–133.

103. One should note two other passages in the prison letters that are interesting regarding Christology, but in both cases it is clear that Bonhoeffer is no longer proposing "theology" but simply reassuring his close friend as to where he is "at" in the matter of faith. In the one he says: "If Jesus had not lived, then our life would be meaningless, in spite of all the other people whom we know and honour and love. Perhaps we now

sometimes forget the meaning and purpose of our profession." (*LPP,* p. 391; August 21, 1944.) And in the other, his last letter to Bethge, he says: "You must never doubt that I'm travelling with gratitude and cheerfulness along the road where I'm being led. My past life is brim-full of God's goodness, and my sins are covered by the forgiving love of Christ crucified." (*LPP,* p. 393; August 23, 1944.)

104. *LPP,* pp. 360–361.

105. *Ibid.,* p. 326 (June 8, 1944).

106. *Ibid.,* p. 337 (June 27, 1944).

107. *Ibid.,* p. 351.

108. Phillips, *Christ for Us . . . ,* p. 96.

109. *Ibid.,* p. 252 (*Die mündige Welt,* Vol. I, p. 122.) Barth was *not* critical of this accent in Bonhoeffer but asked, with some concern, whether "the whole of theology was to be put on this basis."

110. Regin Prenter, "Bonhoeffer and the Young Luther," in R. Gregor Smith (ed.), *World Come of Age,* pp. 161–181. (*Die mündige Welt,* Vol. I, pp. 32–51).

111. Hans Schmidt's assertion that "the 'Cross of Reality' led to a misunderstanding of the cross of Jesus Christ" is a provocative observation in this connection; cf. Hans Schmidt, "The Cross of Reality?" in R. Gregor Smith (ed.), *World Come of Age,* p. 253.

112. Two examples of deficiency in this regard are Feil's failure to note the shift in the meaning and significance of suffering between *The Cost of Discipleship* and *Ethics* and also his dubious assertion that Bonhoeffer's later adoption of the Dilthey world view is purely an objective appraisal and not related to the question of personal development.

113. *Ethics,* p. 194.

114. *Ibid.,* p. 228; cf. also pp. 69–70.

115. Cf. Rasmussen, *Dietrich Bonhoeffer,* p. 24.

116. Lehmann, "Faith and Worldliness in Bonhoeffer's Thought," *loc. cit.,* p. 38.

117. Dumas, *DBTR,* p. 231.

118. See above, p. 27.

119. Bonhoeffer's rejection of Barth's "positivism of revelation" is perhaps best understood in these terms, despite the many more detailed analyses of what might be involved in this. Cf. Helmut Gollwitzer's similar observation on this matter in Zimmermann and Smith (eds.), *I Knew Dietrich Bonhoeffer,* p. 140.

5. COMPLICATION OF THE QUEST:
THE ARISTOCRATIC, VITALISTIC MOTIF

1. John Godsey, "Theologian, Christian, Contemporary," *Interpretation,* Vol. XXV, No. 2 (April 1971), p. 211.

2. Quoted by Bethge, *DB* (E.T.), p. 114.

3. Paul L. Lehmann, "Dietrich Bonhoeffer," unpublished lecture (Union Theological Seminary, 1968), p. 3. Bonhoeffer's fascination with the bullfight was a continuing one; cf. Bethge, *DB* (E.T.), p. 73.

4. It is to be hoped that this point does not need expansion: in speaking of Bonhoeffer's fascination with the vital we are suggesting a close tie between the vitalistic motif and aristocratic tendencies, since the latter draw heavily upon natural force and strength as a major factor in proven worth.

5. Zimmermann and Smith (eds.), *I Knew Dietrich Bonhoeffer,* p. 124. Cf. Bethge, *DB* (E.T.), p. 22; Sabine Leibholz-Bonhoeffer, *The Bonhoeffers: Portrait of a Family* (St. Martin's Press, 1972), p. 39.

6. *Ibid.,* p. 125.

7. Bethge, *DB* (E.T.), pp. 22–23. For a picture of the family environment that seems to have fostered outward discipline and reserve while affirming a vital expression of life, see Bethge, *DB* (E.T.), pp. 4–14, especially pp. 4, 5, 9, 11, 13; Leibholz-Bonhoeffer, *The Bonhoeffers,* pp. 11–12. Numerous attestations to Bonhoeffer's aristocratic bearing and his charismatic presence are to be found in Zimmermann and Smith (eds.), *I Knew Dietrich Bonhoeffer.*

8. Dutch theologian G. T. Rothuizen, in his *Aristocratisch Christendom Over Dietrich Bonhoeffer* (Kampen: J. H. Kok, 1969), has, unlike other interpreters, made Bonhoeffer's aristocratic orientation a major point of departure in his interpretation of Bonhoeffer's thought. This question is certainly, as Rothuizen maintains, of central importance. But whereas Rothuizen is favorably inclined toward Bonhoeffer's proposal of an "aristocratic Christianity" (within some limits), the present writer is very critical of such a formulation.

9. Ott, *Reality and Faith,* p. 106.

10. See *ibid.,* pp. 101–110, for the whole of Ott's argument.

11. *Ibid.,* p. 110.

12. Phillips, *Christ for Us . . . ,* p. 23.

13. *Ibid.* Actually Phillips misquotes Barth in this context and seems

to miss a major point in Barth's description of Bonhoeffer as one "who seemed to run on ahead in the most varied dimensions" (cf. *ibid.,* p. 250). Also Phillips does not here account for a major point in his own analysis, i.e., the assertion that the pressures of the church struggle curtailed the development of Bonhoeffer's "new" (1932) Christology.

14. Mayer, *Christuswirklichkeit,* pp. 224–225.

15. *Ibid.,* p. 225.

16. *Die mündige Welt,* Vol. I, p. 40. Ebeling—earlier than Mayer— makes the point that "in the Tegel letters, of course, when Bonhoeffer speaks of the non-religious man he is not thinking at all of an explicitly anti-religious type like Bolshevism even if that is *a priori* excluded from his mind. What he has in view is rather modern man as such, as represented, e.g., by the 'non-religious working man' . . . but perhaps much more sharply by the type of well-educated, aristocratic middle class, conscious of its public responsibilities and well grounded in tradition—in other words, the class from which Bonhoeffer himself came. We must surely think of certain impressive figures from the resistance movement group—or let us say more generally, of the non-religious man in his noblest and most genuine representatives—if we are to understand what Bonhoeffer meant." (Ebeling, *Word and Faith,* pp. 131–132.)

17. See above, note 8 of this chapter.

18. See above, note 103 of Chapter 4.

19. *LPP,* p. 391.

20. *Ibid.,* p. 392. One should note that the New Testament passages cited here chiefly stress "be strong in the Lord," or "in grace"; only I Cor. 16.13 exhorts "be strong." In the letter of July 8, 1944, Bonhoeffer speaks also of the "sins of weakness" and the "sins of strength" in connection with the figures of Goethe and Napoleon (*ibid.,* p. 345).

21. *Ibid.,* p. 384.

22. *Ibid.,* p. 375.

23. *Ibid.,* p. 371. One should note that the "commandment" in this case is a "contextual" one.

24. *Ibid.,* pp. 344–345.

25. *Ibid.,* p. 326.

26. *Ibid.*

27. *Ibid.,* p. 346.

28. *Ibid.,* pp. 278–282, 285–287, 310–312, 324–329, 335–337, 339–342, 357–361.

29. *Ibid.,* pp. 361–362.

30. *Ibid.,* p. 362.

31. *Ibid.,* p. 370.

32. *Ibid.,* p. 375.

33. In *Ethics* there are still strong strains of the relational "I-Thou" definition of faith, the idea that it is Christ who commands and charges one with responsibility (*Ethics,* pp. 47, 51, 53–54). In the later prison letters, faith becomes more an awareness of identification with the pattern of Christ's life, a recapitulation, it seems, of that life and a variation of the imitation of Christ.

34. *LPP,* pp. 360–361.

35. *Ibid.,* pp. 136, 146, 157–158, 162, 167–168, 191–192, 203, 204–205, 212–213, 217, 232, 233–234.

36. *Ibid.,* p. 229.

37. *Ibid.,* pp. 193–194.

38. *GS* III, pp. 478–495.

39. *LPP,* p. 6.

40. *Ibid.,* p. 13. Bonhoeffer writes in regard to "the sense of quality": "In other times it may have been the business of Christianity to champion the equality of all men; its business today will be to defend passionately human dignity and reserve. Nobility arises from and exists by sacrifice, courage, and a clear sense of duty to oneself and society, by expecting due regard for itself as a matter of course. . . ." (*Ibid.,* pp. 12–13.)

41. *Ethics,* pp. 271–272; cf. also pp. 273–274.

42. See above, note 1 of Chapter 4.

43. *Ethics,* p. 250.

44. *Ibid.,* p. 251. But cf. p. 274; whether Bonhoeffer's thoughts are consistent here may be questioned.

45. *Ibid.,* p. 288.

46. *Ibid.,* p. 289.

47. *Ibid.*

48. *Ibid.;* cf. also p. 163.

49. *Ibid.,* p. 289.

50. *Ibid.,* pp. 290–291.

51. *Ibid.,* p. 219. It should be noted that Feil puzzles over the frequent quoting of Nietzsche in the *Ethics;* see Feil, *DTDB,* p. 194n21.

52. *Ibid.*

53. *Ibid.*

54. *Ibid.,* pp. 53–54.

55. *Ibid.,* pp. 66–67.

56. *Ibid.,* pp. 120–143; especially pp. 133–143.

57. *Life Together,* p. 39.

58. *Ibid.,* pp. 22–23, 54.

59. Bethge has confirmed the fact that after Bonhoeffer's return from America in 1939 the practice of personal confession between himself and Bonhoeffer ceased. (Eberhard Bethge, personal interview, June 1970.)

60. *Life Together,* pp. 112–115.

61. *Ibid.,* p. 94; cf. *Ethics,* p. 163.

62. *Life Together,* p. 88.

63. *Ibid.,* p. 33.

64. *Ibid.*

65. *Ibid.,* pp. 29, 30, 38, 64, 65, 89, 90–91, 101–102, 104–105, 109.

66. See above, pp. 77–78.

67. *CD,* pp. 40–41.

68. In the "Memoir" prefacing *The Cost of Discipleship,* Gerhard Leibholz, Bonhoeffer's brother-in-law, writes: "The majority of the people in all nations alike does not consist of heroes. What Dietrich Bonhoeffer and others did cannot be expected from the many. The future in modern society depends much more on the quiet heroism of the very few who are inspired by God. These few will greatly enjoy the divine inspiration and will be prepared to stand for the dignity of man and true freedom and to keep the law of God, even if it means martyrdom or death." (*CD,* p. 33.)

69. *CD,* pp. 49–50.

70. *Ibid.,* p. 50.

71. *Ibid.,* pp. 51–52.

72. *Ibid.,* p. 52.

73. *Ibid.*

74. *Ibid.,* p. 55.

75. *Ibid.,* pp. 303–304.

76. *Ibid.,* p. 273; cf. also p. 342.

77. *Ibid.,* pp. 273–274.

78. Cf. *ibid.,* p. 190; also pp. 96, 100–101, 170–171, 273, 342. Also see above, note 78 of Chapter 4.

79. Cf. Otto Michel, "Besprechung," *Theologische Literaturzeitung,* Vol. LXIV, No. 2 (Feb. 1939), cols. 63–66.

80. For passages that reflect the spiritually autobiographical, see *CD,* pp. 60, 173, 212, 214, 217, 239, 242, 249–253, 289, 330–333. Bonhoeffer's 1936 letter to Barth mentioning work on *The Cost of Discipleship* illuminates Bonhoeffer's own spiritual search; cf. Dietrich Bonhoeffer, *The Way*

to Freedom (Harper & Row, Publishers, Inc., 1966), pp. 116–118 (*GS* II, pp. 284–286). Cf. also Bonhoeffer's first letter to Barth in December 1932, *NRS*, pp. 204–205 (*GS* II, pp. 39–40).

81. *The Communion of Saints*, pp. 54, 58–59, 60, 130–131, 189, especially p. 143.

82. *Act and Being*, pp. 28, 141, 158–159, 160, 167–168, 176–177. This argument does not deny what Feil observes about Bonhoeffer's shift in *Act and Being* from the *actus reflexus* to the *actus directus*, except to point out a not insignificant flaw in Feil's argument as a whole. It should be noted that this shift from the *actus reflexus* to the *actus directus* is not simply a matter of hermeneutics relating to the question of the "who" of God and the content of the Biblical materials; it has great, if not greater meaning, in the anthropological realm—that is, in Bonhoeffer's own quest for identity. On this point see Bonhoeffer's discussion of "Man in Contemporary Philosophy and Theology," his inaugural lecture at the University of Berlin, July 31, 1930, delivered after completion of *Act and Being* (*NRS*, pp. 50–69, especially p. 65; *GS* III, pp. 62–84). On this same point one must take cognizance of the fact that the whole matter of the "hiddenness" of God (cf. *Christ the Center*, pp. 28–29, 30–31, 46–47, 64, 106, 110–111, 117–118), while constituting a major point in Bonhoeffer's polemic against idealism (a dimension of the Barthian logic), also carries a potential for anthropological development. And one must ask if this is not what happens to Bonhoeffer's later thought when the statement of "the secret" and "the hidden" is developed primarily on anthropological grounds in conjunction with Bonhoeffer's "aristocratic Christianity" (see especially the letter of July 8, 1944, *LPP*, pp. 343–347). Cf. also Bonhoeffer's frequent accent on "secret discipline," "reticence," "the sense of reserve."

83. *NRS*, p. 44.

84. Bethge, "The Challenge of Dietrich Bonhoeffer's Life and Theology," *loc. cit.*, p. 4.

85. It goes without saying that this analysis departs markedly from one offered by Bethge; see *DB* (E.T.), pp. 85–87, 773.

86. See above, note 78 of Chapter 4 and n. 33 of this chapter.

87. See below, p. 129.

88. Feil, *DTDB*, p. 131.

89. *Ibid.*, p. 370.

90. Cf. Bethge, *DB* (E.T.), pp. 153–156.

91. Feil, *DTDB*, p. 74n18; cf. Bethge, *DB* (E.T.), pp. 112–113, 138.

92. Feil, *DTDB*, p. 129.

93. *Ibid.*, pp. 72–80.

94. *Ibid.*, pp. 81–126, 127–133.

95. See above, pp. 74–75.

96. *LPP*, p. 318.

97. Feil, *DTDB*, pp. 74–75. Feil also underlines Bonhoeffer's desire to serve in the pastorate.

98. Bethge, *DB* (E.T.), p. 230.

99. *NRS*, pp. 204–205.

100. *Ibid.*, p. 234.

101. *Ibid.*, p. 235.

102. *Ibid.*, p. 236.

103. See Bethge, *DB* (E.T.), pp. 231–234.

104. *NRS*, p. 238.

105. An anti–"German Christian" group whose members were, in Barth's eyes, flagging in their commitment.

106. *NRS*, p. 238.

107. *Ibid.*, p. 239.

108. *Ibid.*, p. 240.

109. See Bethge, *DB* (E.T.), pp. 254–340.

110. *The Way to Freedom*, pp. 115–116.

111. *Ibid.*, p. 116.

112. *Ibid.*, p. 117.

113. *Ibid.*, p. 118.

114. *Ibid.*, p. 119.

115. *Ibid.*, p. 121.

116. It is not clear that Bonhoeffer's description to Sutz of this last Barth correspondence is what Bonhoeffer actually felt about it. Cf. *GS* I, p. 46.

117. *NRS*, p. 120–121, 140.

118. Bethge, *DB* (E.T.), pp. 538–539.

119. *The Way to Freedom*, p. 206. Later, in an effort to explain his sudden decision to return to Germany, Bonhoeffer told his American friends of the need for teachers in the Confessing Church; cf. *ibid.*, pp. 242–243.

120. *Ibid.*, p. 210; *GS* I, p. 286.

121. *Ibid.*, p. 211; *GS* I, p. 287–288.

122. Bethge, *DB* (E.T.), pp. 540–542, 544, 552–553.

123. *The Way to Freedom*, p. 218.

124. Bethge, *DB* (E.T.), pp. 552–553.

125. *The Way to Freedom,* pp. 214–217.
126. *Ibid.,* p. 217.
127. *Ibid.,* pp. 228–229.
128. *Ibid.,* p. 230.
129. *Ibid.,* p. 233.
130. *Ibid.,* p. 238.
131. *Ibid.*
132. *Ibid.,* p. 246.
133. *Ibid.,* p. 247.
134. *Ibid.*
135. *Ibid.*
136. Bethge, *DB* (E.T.), p. 541.
137. *Ibid.,* p. 540.
138. *Ibid.,* p. 552.
139. *Ibid.,* pp. 540–542, 544, 552–553.
140. *Ibid.,* p. 553.
141. *Ibid.,* p. 541.
142. *Ibid.,* p. 338. Italics mine.
143. *Ibid.,* p. 339. The phrasing here recalls Bonhoeffer's definition of the disciple as the one who "simply burns his boats and goes ahead" (*CD,* p. 62).
144. *The Way to Freedom,* p. 230.
145. *Ibid.,* p. 247.
146. Cf. Bethge, *DB* (E.T.), pp. 562–565.
147. *LPP,* pp. 275–276. Cf. Feil, *DTDB,* pp. 129–131; Ott, *Reality and Faith,* pp. 370–371.
148. *LPP,* p. 272.
149. *LPP,* p. 174.
150. *The Way to Freedom,* p. 238. Italics mine.
151. See above, note 59 of this chapter.
152. See above, p. 110.
153. *The Way to Freedom,* p. 238.
154. *GS* I, pp. 323–354.
155. *The Way to Freedom,* p. 250.
156. *Ibid.,* p. 255. Cf. "Stations on the Road to Freedom," *LPP,* pp. 370–371.
157. Bethge, *DB* (E.T.), pp. 565–566; cf. also pp. 156, 273–274.
158. *Ethics,* p. 124. Italics mine. Bonhoeffer tries in this passage also to establish a dialectic with the "now" of the Word of God; but in the

judgment of this writer it is not an authentic dialectic. If the "now" of God's grace were to receive its proper weight, the penultimate would become in part an occasion of rejoicing and not simply a "way to be traversed." Overtones of *The Cost of Discipleship* are to be noted here, but the veil of piety has been dropped and Bonhoeffer is no longer seeking the experience of grace via the method of obedience. He seeks it now by remaining true to the natural, the penultimate. Cf. *LPP*, p. 370.

159. *LPP*, p. 282.
160. Ott, *Reality and Faith*, p. 106.

6. THE NATURE OF THE DISSENT

1. Ebeling, *Word and Faith*, p. 148.
2. *Ibid.*, pp. 148–150.
3. *LPP*, p. 360.
4. *LPP*, pp. 286, 382.
5. *Ibid.*, pp. 286, 328.
6. *Ibid.*, p. 333.
7. *Ibid.*, p. 303.
8. The words "resistance" and "submission" are taken from Bethge's chosen title for the German edition of the prison letters: *Widerstand und Ergebung.*
9. *LPP*, p. 382. The statement recalls Bonhoeffer's 1936 correspondence with Barth and the reference to Tholuck; see above, p. 120.
10. See above, p. 107.
11. Cf. Bethge, *DB* (E.T.), pp. 193–194. The radio speech was subsequently expanded and was delivered at the School for Politics in Berlin in March 1933. Much of what follows comes from the expanded lecture; cf. *GS* II, pp. 22–24.
12. *NRS*, pp. 190–191.
13. *Ibid.*, p. 191.
14. It should be noted in addition that this particular lecture is also surprisingly lacking in theological content.
15. Cf., e.g., Bonhoeffer's first address to an American audience (*NRS*, pp. 76–85).
16. *LPP*, p. 299. The date of this writing is May 1944.
17. Cf. Cox, *The Secular City*, pp. 60–62, 68, 70–78, 79–80, 251–253. Cf. also Peter Berger, "Camus, Bonhoeffer and the World Come of Age," *The Christian Century*, Vol. LXXVI, No. 14 (April 8, 1959), pp. 417–418,

and No. 15 (April 15, 1959), pp. 450–452. One should also note at this point a major reservation regarding Reist's program of an "ethicizing of theology" (cf. Reist, *The Promise of Bonhoeffer,* pp. 118–119). Involvement, even earnest ethical involvement, does not guarantee significant historical insight and understanding; and it is hard to see how theology can be good theology if historical reality, which is also human reality, is not perceptively grasped.

18. *LPP,* pp. 286, 382.

19. To refuse to deny this possibility is one thing, but to want to offer exposition of it would seem to be another.

20. Cf. *LPP,* pp. 286–287, 329, 337, 346, 361, 382. The passage in the letter of July 16 (p. 361) is important in that it indicates how Bonhoeffer's image of a world come of age leads on to "non-religious interpretation."

21. *LPP,* p. 329.

22. Luke 5:31–32 (RSV); cf. Matt. 9:12, 13; Mark 2:17.

23. *LPP,* p. 384.

24. *LPP,* p. 392.

25. *Ibid.,* pp. 341–342.

26. *Ibid.,* p. 327.

27. *Ibid.,* p. 346. Italics mine.

28. Alistair Kee, "I Did Not Know Dietrich Bonhoeffer," *The Christian Century,* Vol. LXXXIX, No. 38 (Oct. 25, 1972), p. 1067.

29. Cf. Reinhold Niebuhr, *Beyond Tragedy: Essays on the Christian Interpretation of History* (Charles Scribner's Sons, 1938), pp. 198–199.

30. James Woelfel in *Bonhoeffer's Theology: Classical and Revolutionary* makes this mixture of elements the theme of his interpretation of Bonhoeffer.

31. *LPP,* p. 387.

32. *Ibid.,* p. 392.

33. *Ibid.,* p. 393.

EPILOGUE

1. John Calvin, *Institutes of the Christian Religion,* I. i. 1–3.

2. Ludwig Feuerbach, *The Essence of Christianity,* tr. by George Eliot (Harper & Row, Publishers, Inc., 1957), p. xxiii.

3. See Barth's own discussion of this matter in Karl Barth, *The Humanity of God* (John Knox Press, 1960).

4. The question of Christ certainly raises the question of anthropology,

but the latter must always be explicitly treated and discussed.

5. And here we have in mind not a "baptizing" of a secular alternative (as, e.g., in Cox's *The Secular City*) but the delineation of a distinctively theological possibility.

6. Feuerbach, *The Essence of Christianity,* p. xxiii.

7. Rudolf Bultmann, *Jesus Christ and Mythology* (Charles Scribner's Sons, 1958), p. 71.

8. Cf. *LPP,* p. 373.

9. Søren Kierkegaard, *Fear and Trembling* and *The Sickness Unto Death,* tr. by Walter Lowrie (Princeton University Press, 1968), p. 83.

10. See above, pp. 136–138.

Index